Mondays with My Old Pastor

"Every now and then I come across a book I can't get out of my head. *Mondays with My Old Pastor* is one of those books. I guarantee you'll be thinking about it long after you put it down."

— **Andy Andrews**
New York Times best-selling
author of *How Do You Kill 11
Million People?*; *The Noticer*; and
The Traveler's Gift

"*Mondays with My Old Pastor* brings us face to face with the frequent disappointments of our Christian journey, while offering us a wonderful encounter between two pastors: one who has faithfully finished his career with perseverance, and another who is just beginning. The counsel of the elder strengthens the spirit of the young one as he sends him back on his way. It will probably do the same for those struggling with the same disappointments who read this captivating work of José Luis Navajo."

— **Eugenio Orellana**
Founder and International
Director, Latin American
Association of Christian
Writers

"*Mondays with My Old Pastor* qualifies as a pastor peer support group all its own. Research bears out the experience of the book's narrator: approximately 10 percent of clergy are depressed at any given time, and all clergy are challenged to balance competing demands. This books passes on helpful wisdom and the comfort of shared experience."

— **Rae Jean Proeschold-Bell, PhD**
Research Director of the Duke
Clergy Health Initiative

"There are few books I read that make it to my favorite pile. But *Mondays with My Old Pastor* now sits among those books. There is so much wisdom to savor in its pages . . . so much important conversation in every chapter. It is for the discouraged minister, the questioning spiritual soldier, and every believer in between. The words from Jose Luis Navajo's old pastor's lips are Jesus-words, and I felt every one."

— **Lisa Whittle**
Author, Speaker, Advocate

Mondays

WITH

My Old Pastor

Sometimes, all we need is a reminder from
someone who has walked before us

José Luis Navajo

THOMAS NELSON
Since 1798

NASHVILLE DALLAS MEXICO CITY RIO DE JANEIRO

Published in Nashville, Tennessee, by Thomas Nelson. Thomas Nelson is a registered trademark of Thomas Nelson, Inc.

Thomas Nelson, Inc. titles may be purchased in bulk for educational, business, fund-raising, or sales promotional use. For information, please e-mail SpecialMarkets@ThomasNelson.com.

Unless otherwise marked, Scripture quotations are taken from the New King James Version®. © 1982 by Thomas Nelson, Inc. Used by permission. All rights reserved.

Scripture quotations marked NIV are taken from the Holy Bible, New International Version®, NIV®. © 1973, 1978, 1984, 2011 by Biblica, Inc.™ Used by permission of Zondervan. All rights reserved worldwide. www.zondervan.com

Some of the stories in this book are legends or myths that are not true but are used to illustrate a point.

Library of Congress Cataloging-in-Publication Data

Navajo, José Luis.
   Mondays with my old pastor / Jos? Luis Navajo.
      p. cm.
   Includes bibliographical references (p.   ).
   ISBN 978-0-8499-4725-4 (trade paper)
   1. Clergy—Appointment, call, and election. 2. Vocation, Ecclesiastical. 3. Pastoral theology. 4. Vocation—Christianity. 5. Career changes. 6. Burn-out (Psychology)—Religious aspects—Christianity. I. Title.
   BV4011.4.N38 2012
   253.2—dc23   2011053193

Printed in the United States of America

12 13 14 15 16 QG 5 4 3 2 1

To Querit

*Your smile lights up a thousand lights
during my discouraged times.*

To Miriam

*Every day you show us that adolescence also
has magical treasures that we as parents can
enjoy. Amazed at your maturity, I sometimes ask
myself, "Is she my daughter or my mother?"*

And to you, Gene

*Your unshakable love, closeness, and loyalty weave together
the threads that hold my comet of hope high in the sky.*

Contents

Acknowledgments

I would not have been able to write this story without the people who inspired it.

To the thousands of men and women who with great dedication take care of the small "parcel of land" where God has planted them: thank you for digging your feet in and getting your hands dirty in the clay of this holy work.

I give my heartfelt thanks to Thomas Nelson and their excellent staff for believing in this humble work and for helping it come to life. My wish is that this child of paper and ink brings happiness and blessing to many lives.

Prologue

A few weeks ago, I celebrated my forty-sixth birthday.

Despite the fact that I would have preferred not seeing so many candles on the cake, it was a nice day. There were surprises, hugs, and an abundance of sincere affection. What more could one ask for?

Nothing was missing, not even unwrapping a beautiful gift to discover that it contained *exactly what I needed!* Yet not even the joyful singing of "Happy Birthday," which was sung out of tune and not in rhythm, thrilled me.

At the end of the day, while I was picking up the wrapping paper from the gifts and putting the leftover cake in the refrigerator, I couldn't stop asking myself, "Why do I feel this way even on my birthday?"

Deep in some uncertain part of my soul persisted a strange exhaustion that was difficult to explain and hard to endure. I'm referring to something that is greater than mere tiredness. It has more to do with emotions rather than muscles. It is more related to the soul rather than the body.

I am an evangelical pastor, and for some time I had felt . . . how can I explain it? I can't seem to find the exact word to describe it.

Let down?

No, not at all.

Disillusioned?

No, not that either.

Tired?

Yes, I believe that's it . . . or something similar.

Please understand me; I'm not saying that I've taken the wrong road in life. If I were to be born all over again, if God were to give me the gift of another life, I would ask Him to let me make the same investment—the exact same one I have made with the years that He has given me up until now. That is not presumption. It's gratitude.

Many believe that being called by God to serve Him in ministry is the highest privilege and the noblest opportunity. I believe that as well.

Some say that in their whole life they never have had the thought of leaving Christian ministry to devote themselves to something else. I would love to claim that I belong to that elite group. I wish I could assure you that I have never felt overwhelmed by the desire to hang up my gloves, or throw in the towel, or whatever we call looking at the plow stuck in the furrow and longing for softer soil or greener fields. I wish I could assure you of that, but I wouldn't be honest if I did.

Thirty-five years ago, I was given the honor of digging my feet into the soil of this sacred work, and even until today, only two other passions captivate me more than God's work: the God of the work and my family.

But we would be doing little favor to those who are willing to take up the baton and relieve us in this race, if when we show them the path, we only emphasize the oases and forget to mention the deserts.

To be called by God is, beyond any doubt, the highest vocation to which someone can aspire. But serving Him implies entering a battle, and it is wise to remember that in a battle there are no soldiers without wounds. It is normal for discouragement to come at times, and it happened to me.

The pages that you are about to read were not written all at once but rather came about over time, by a process that led me through some very unique moments.

At times I was able to dip my pen in the "ink" of God's heart, but at other times, the ink was blood that sprang from my own wounds. Some lines were edited by the light of a rainbow, while others were birthed from the roar of uncomfortable thoughts, some of which shouted, *It would be better if I devoted myself to something else. I don't have a career; it was all a wild fancy, a false hope; this life isn't for me.*

The pressure got so bad that one day I thought I was dying, and I had no choice but to see the doctor. I tried to explain to him the gibberish that was going on in my mind, which was causing serious ramifications in my soul and severe problems in my body. Since I didn't know what was happening to me, I was guessing at what it all meant. The kind doctor listened to me with commendable patience, keeping his elbows on the table, his fingers locked together, and his head resting on both thumbs.

Finally, he looked at me with a frank smile, which made me

relax at times and made me uncomfortable other times. Then he shelled out his diagnosis: burnout.

Burnout? The one who runs nonstop soon drops? The one who fires off his twenty-year supply of ammunition in twenty days? The one who forces his horse to run so hard he wears him out?

I didn't know what he was talking about!

Things such as "grabbing more reins of the convenient" and "galloping bareback on several horses is complicated and makes it easy for them to get out of hand." Crowding too many matters together on the journey puts an unbearable weight on a person.

He was so emphatic and persuasive that I had to admit that perhaps he was right.

When he had finished with his diagnosis, he stared at me again with his unchanging smile and gave me his orders: "I am prescribing mandatory rest for you," he said, with the same ease as if he had prescribed an aspirin.

Thankfully, I have not had to experience what is known as forced labor, though I have a deep respect for those who have found themselves in that spot. But I can attest to the fact that "mandatory rest" isn't easy.

It wasn't the first time that my frail nature forced me to come to a stop—at times I have come to the conclusion that God has gifted me with bad health just so I can write. He knew full well that from that moment on I would be facing my fiercest enemy in my mind, because when the body slows down, the mind begins to race nonstop.

So I decided to quickly cut off that kind of thinking before I became a prisoner to it. Taking advantage of the mandatory rest,

I was able come to a powerful conclusion: it is possible—I know now—to "cook" so feverishly for God that we end up kicking Him out of the kitchen. Yes, that's possible, but it is absolutely unwise to do so.

A difficult yoke and a heavy weight do not fit the description Jesus gave of His commission; on the contrary, those two things can set us on such a steep uphill climb that it makes us feel like giving up.

Has that ever happened to you? Have you thought that at one time or another?

Don't torment or judge yourself too harshly.

Welcome to the club.

A wise man once said, "You can't keep the birds from flying over your head, but you can sure keep them from building a nest in your hair!" As I captured the reflections that sprang from my heart with one hand, and with the other hand scared away the ugly blackbirds that tried to build nests in the crevices of my mind, I wrote many pages of this book.

Would you like to travel through this journey with me? Together we will prove that as we hold on to God in this dark cave, we will always come out the other side; and we will emerge on higher ground, with a greater vision under a clearer and calmer sky.

I am confident in saying that at some point in your reading you will stop and realize that the darkest hour of the night is the one that comes just before the dawn, and that there is no winter—no matter how harsh and long it may seem—that doesn't turn into a lush spring.

I am sure that before you reach the last page, you will have proven that the deepest crises are often shortcuts to greater opportunities, and the blows you have received on God's anvil don't destroy but rather build up.

If you have come this far in your reading, I congratulate you, because now the really interesting part begins.

I want to introduce you to my old pastor so that together you and I can walk through the rooms of his humble, whitewashed home in the desert and find the powerful cross that is being lifted up among the dunes.

—José Luis Navajo

"Did you know, son, that when I was a little boy I used to spend hours listening to my father? Oh, how I remember the wisdom that came from his words! Listening to him, I could feel myself grow. He used to shake off the dusty archives of his memory to pass on to me beautiful thoughts and valuable lessons."

The honorable grandfather paused, moved by nostalgia, and then he finished: "What a pity that today old men are not so wise that you can learn by listening to us!"

The young man took the old man's hands in his, and looking him in the eyes, he said, "That's not it at all, Father. If we don't spend time listening to you, it's not because you're less wise. Rather, it's because we are much more foolish."

The father cracked a smile that radiated pure love and then kissed his son's cheek, just before hugging him.

Wisdom is with aged men,
And with length of days, understanding.
—JOB 12:12

Introduction

A Cross in the Desert

I stopped in front of the whitewashed house protected from the sun by a climbing vine. *So this is my old pastor's refuge?* I thought as I gazed at that humble building.

As I slowly walked the few feet that separated me from the door, two feelings—shyness and insecurity—equally overwhelmed me.

In an attempt to find the courage to knock on the door, I forced myself to remember the determination with which my old pastor had urged me to come and visit him.

"I don't know . . ." I hesitantly had told him on the phone. "I wouldn't want to bother you . . ."

"Don't say another word. Come this Monday"—it was the third time that he insisted—"I really want to see you and give you a hug."

Because of that, I was now standing in front of that blue door studded with black nails. I couldn't get rid of the feeling that I was nothing more than a meddler who had only come to disturb the deserved rest of the old man who offered to bestow on me the gift of his time.

But the memory of the crippling circumstances that had brought me here was enough incentive for my hand to grab the bronze knocker in the center of the door that served to announce my arrival.

Let me give you a little background of my most recent turn of events:

I had dedicated my life in service to God, to which I gave myself completely. However, lately things had suffered some changes.

I had become discouraged.

Definitely and absolutely discouraged.

The feeling of knowing that I couldn't do anything, that I didn't know anything, and that I wasn't useful at all had completely overwhelmed me.

I was fulfilling—or, at least, I was trying to fulfill—my pastoral responsibilities in a small church in a tiny town. Everything about it was small. But that responsibility seemed so huge to me and, above all, so hard that it threatened to crush me.

One Sunday, after arriving home from church, I shut myself in my room and knelt with my elbows on the bed. Burying my face in my hands, I prayed and cried for a long time, but I felt as if it all was in vain. Even my prayer seemed useless to me. My words seemed to crash against the ceiling and then fall back down on me, turned into a shower of splinters that were being hammered into my hunched back.

After praying and crying, I remained on my knees waiting for something. But nothing happened.

The following day I caved in. I gave up—at least in my heart. I wanted to stop serving God because I felt morally bankrupt. I was unable to resist, so I sank into discouragement.

Everything happened right there, in that moment, one sunny Monday in the beginning of May.

Had I lost my faith?

I wasn't sure, but since I certainly had lost my love, I no longer had the same amount of desire as when I had started the race.

When I got on board the boat of service to God, I did it full of projects and dreams. That was nine years ago. It was a particularly long "pregnancy." And the resulting birth produced triplets: discouragement, frustration, and disillusionment.

Consequently, the little boat I had excitedly climbed into was now filling up with water everywhere, while the raging sea of discouragement was threatening to swallow me up.

I started to examine each year of my life as a regrettable and senseless mistake. And I saw what time I still had left as a colorless void that I had no desire to spiral down into.

I've experienced crises at other times, but not so profound or so sudden.

It didn't take long for my wife, Mary, to pick up on my feelings. That's not strange. She is able to read my eyes and with one look x-ray my whole soul.

"What's going on with you, sweetheart?"

Her support is unconditional, and her faith in me is as well;

but not even a life jacket as amazing as hers seemed strong enough in the fierce sea that threatened to swallow me.

"Tell me," she insisted. "What's wrong?"

"Nothing," I said to her. I even tried to silence her lips with a kiss to stop the floodgate of sincere questions I didn't know how to respond to.

"Nothing's wrong. Don't worry."

Being respectful as she was, she would abide her time until she knew that the intense storm, which could not last long, had passed.

A few weeks like this went by: plunged in a tunnel of discouragement, fighting against the overwhelming feeling of being incapable of doing anything, of not knowing what to do, and not feeling useful. With each passing moment I even toyed with the possibility of leaving the ministry and devoting myself to something else.

I don't have a calling, I thought. *Everything is just a pipe dream, a false hope. This life is not for me.*

"Why don't you talk to your old pastor?" my wife suggested one night after I had answered her question with the same evasive answer as always.

"With my old pastor?"

"Yes."

She smiled at me with her sweet expression that was a healing balm for my wounds. "Why don't you go and talk to him?"

The term *old* was not used to refer to our pastor with disrespect, but with sincere affection and true admiration. In his golden years we never saw the wear and tear of his age, but rather the incalculable value of his experience.

He was a seasoned eighty-three years old—fifty-five of those he had dedicated to pastoring the same church—and every day that had gone by had deposited in him another drop in the well of wisdom.

His life was a confirmation of Ingmar Bergman's reflection, when he said, "Old age is like climbing a large mountain. The higher you get, the more tired and breathless you become, but your sight becomes more free and the view more extensive and serene."

It had only been a few months since he had retired. He and his wife, Rachel, had decided to flee from all the noise and spend the last stretch of their journey in prayer and seclusion.

"We have served Him on the front line, and now we want to set ourselves apart with Him," he had said the day of their farewell. "For fifty-five years we have spoken to people about God. Now we long to speak to God about people."

"Why don't you give your old pastor a call?" Mary repeated, snapping me out of my daydreaming.

I did not answer, and she was fine with that. She knew that my silence was a promise that I would take her suggestion into consideration. And that's exactly what I did. I took her advice to bed with me and turned over a thousand times with it, until I finally fell asleep.

I almost never dream, but that night I dreamed.

I saw myself in the middle of a desert, languishing under scorching heat. My skin was on fire, and the sun's rays beat down like knives that tore open my reddened flesh. My lips were very dry and cracked. Exhausted, I fell to the ground.

With superhuman effort, I succeeded in standing up and managed to move forward a few inches before falling down again.

Finally, my legs refused to move, so I gave up and stretched out on the sand, convinced I was going to die.

Just when a deadly slumber started to engulf me, a refreshing shade covered me. The temperature dropped a few degrees, and even my hair stirred from a breeze that was as strange as it was invigorating. I felt revived. It felt like the soft embrace of a silk sheet after a hard day at work. Where did the shade come from? I raised my eyes and had to rub them to convince myself that what I was seeing wasn't a mirage: a large cross had been lifted up in that scorching land, placing itself between the sun and my fallen body.

Its shade stretched directly over me. An irresistible attraction drew me toward it, and I could see a human figure smiling at me from the foot of the cross. It was someone, kneeling, who was pointing at me with one hand, while with the other he was pointing toward the huge cross that had been lifted up in the heart of the desert. Digging my fingers into the sand, I succeeded in dragging myself a little closer.

I could only see a little bit, but enough to recognize the person who was calling to me. It was my old pastor! Renewed by the coolness that flowed from the shade of the cross, I felt something akin to peace. Suddenly, from within the cloud of almost total darkness I felt inside, his voice broke through. He said, "In returning and rest you shall be saved; in quietness and confidence shall be your strength." A soft yet powerful voice; extraordinary but imbued with power. Totally unique.

With the echo of that voice in my mind and my pajama shirt stuck to my body, I woke up with a jolt. I had absolutely no doubt: that dream confirmed that Mary's advice was wise and well-timed.

And that's why I was standing in front of the blue door of that simple whitewashed house.

Silence was the predominant music of this incredibly fertile but extremely unpopulated place. No other house could be seen anywhere nearby. That house had been built in the middle of nowhere. Its foundations had been laid out in total isolation, and it was protected by the most perfect peace. The stone floor and the walls were covered in flower petals—red, white, and pink—that fell down from the circular ledge that was full of flowerpots, and from the two balconies.

On both sides of the door sat two large tubs filled with roses, which I bent down to smell. They were pure white, and their petals held drops of water that looked like tiny crystals.

I took a few steps back to admire the simple but imposing structure of that house, and then I noticed one small detail: the chimney that rose up several feet, along with the outline of the tiled roof, cast a shadow that formed the exact shape of a cross.

I kept my eyes riveted on the scene for more than a minute. It was a perfect cross, made enormously long by the setting sun.

An identical cross to the one in my dream.

A cross in the desert . . .

From that moment on, one of the most dizzying and extraordinary periods I had ever experienced began.

For months I did not understand what was happening, and only now can I recount it with certain conviction, because the passage of time has caused me to understand that in every desert there is a cross that brings restoration. It's only a question of looking for it and taking shelter in its shade.

Sometimes we don't even have the strength to look for it . . . but the cross will find us, and we will prove that the hottest place will be transformed into a fertile garden.

The First Monday

Angels in the Desert

Only God exists, only God knows, only God is able . . .
Only God is the true wise One.

Fearful, taking one slow step after another, I reached the door of the house. And what I saw left me astonished.

Next to the right lintel, hanging from the facade, was a reddish stone shaped like a piece of parchment. On the stone were inscribed the words of the prophet: "In returning and rest you shall be saved; in quietness and confidence shall be your strength" (Isaiah 30:15).

The very same words that woke me up from my dream were now right in front of my eyes.

I could hardly believe it.

As I breathed in deeply the restful and fragrant air, I thought, *I can see that my old pastor and his wife have fulfilled their wish. They found a place to rest and trust.* I knew, without a doubt, that they had turned this quietude into an altar and that sacred silence into worship.

When I arrived at my pastor's house to visit him the first of June, my intention was to have coffee together and let him know how I was feeling.

Just before I knocked on the door, I realized that it was Monday, like the first Monday of May, which was the day I had given up. Little did I also realize that this sunny Monday, the first day of June, would be the beginning of my restoration!

One more step and I would cross over that threshold, initiating a radical change in my life. A decisive time was about to commence.

The sun showered down from an unbelievably blue sky, and its heat cascaded over each side of the house. Not one leaf was moving when, slowly, I grabbed the sizzling bronze door-knocker and let it knock on the door two times.

With the soft sound of footsteps, it was kindhearted Rachel, my old pastor's constant and faithful companion, who opened the door for me. Surprised to see me, she spoke my name and let me know she was happy to see me. She greeted me with a kiss on each cheek and let me pass with a beaming smile as she said warmly, "Welcome!"

My old pastor was already approaching through the hallway. "Hello," he shouted, raising his arms and extending them toward me. "It brings me great joy to see you here in my house."

In the midst of that suffocating heat, a breeze of affection enveloped me. There was neither feigning nor pretense in his happiness. His friendly hug conveyed the most sincere welcome.

I was already feeling better.

The warm reception by those two angels had an instantaneous therapeutic effect. I felt that even if the visit had ended right then, I still would have returned home comforted.

Looking at them, I became convinced that it is wrinkles of the spirit that make us old, not wrinkles on the face. I sensed in them two souls overflowing with youthfulness and authentic vitality. *What is it they have,* I asked myself, *that just their presence inspires encouragement?*

The inside of the house was just as simple as the outside suggested.

As soon as we entered, we gained access to a short entryway from which four doors opened. The one to the right led to a small kitchen that contained all the basics, including a door that opened to a porch with a table and four chairs.

I envisioned them sitting there, sipping their early-morning coffee and delighting in the vast nature that stretched out before them.

Above the sink was a large window covered with a lace curtain, but it did not block the view of the hundred-year-old oak tree that stretched its branches over the house as if wanting to provide shelter from the early summer sun.

The door in front of the kitchen led into a small but cozy parlor. Two rockers were turned toward a blackened fireplace, a sign of many winters spent enjoying its heat and intimacy.

Between the two rockers stood a low table on which rested a

Bible, whose well-worn cover bore the words *Large Print*. It was the one he was using lately, since his eyes had lost their keenness, even though the glow of his determination had never been extinguished.

Then I noticed one detail: a large cross was embossed on the cover of the Bible. From there my eyes jumped to the old log beams that rested above the home. They also formed a cross. Next I noticed that the wall shelves, filled with pictures and mementos, were designed precisely with the same shape. The same pattern occurred in the windowpanes of the large window, where two white wooden strips of wood between two panes of glass formed a cross.

My old pastor noticed what I had seen.

"Ah, you see it, don't you?" he asked me with a smile. "The cross."

"Yes, it's everywhere. What does it mean?"

His smile at that moment was filled with more light than the purest late-afternoon sun on that cloudless day.

"My life has sprung forth from the shade of the cross. I have always lived protected by it, and I want the cross to be the ladder that lifts me up to His presence when my time comes."

"What is it that you find in it?" I dared to ask him.

He only thought for a few seconds before answering. "I find Him," he said, pointing upward with his index finger. "I find Him in the cross, nothing more, nothing less. What more can you ask for?"

I stared at a stairway in the corner of the living room that led upstairs, where the bedrooms were most certainly located. The third door in the hallway led to a small bathroom that was just as clean as the rest of the house.

Only one more door remained, which my old pastor was pointing toward.

"I will bring you both some coffee right away," Rachel promised as she headed toward the kitchen.

That room was his office.

Two things caught my attention immediately: the huge floor-to-ceiling bookshelf that covered an entire wall, into which were crowded hundreds of books; and the large window that was to the right of his study desk. That large window provided an enchanting view. The countryside stretched out as far as the eye could see, and now, in full spring, the grass looked like a succulent carpet that covered the ground in a brilliant, almost phosphorescent, green.

Looking at the bookshelf crammed with books, I remembered the advice my old pastor had given me once: "You should read a lot, especially the Bible, but also seek to soak yourself with wisdom from others. A good book will make you grow. They are like mines," he had said to me, as he fondly caressed the book in his hands. "Mines full of riches. Each chapter is a like a showcase that is hiding treasures, waiting for someone to discover them."

I glanced at the book spines, trying to make out the titles.

"One thousand seven hundred and twelve," he told me.

"Excuse me?"

"One thousand seven hundred and twelve books, in alphabetical order and annotated in hand-penned lists." He smiled. "You know that I have always been a compulsive reader."

"And an extremely organized person," I acknowledged. "And for sure, many of us were infected with your passion for reading."

He sat down in a wing-back chair that was facing the large

window. I surmised that this must be his favorite spot. To his side stood a low table with a lamp.

I thought of the idyllic times my old pastor must have spent sitting in that chair, gazing through the window during the day and contemplating the wide-open green landscape . . . and worshipping in the glimmering light of the lamp at night.

"Thank you for granting me a few minutes of your time," I told him somewhat timidly, taking a seat in front of him.

"You're thanking me?" he said, smiling more with his eyes than his mouth. "I'm the one who should be thankful. Since I've been retired I have plenty of time, and I haven't had many occasions to enjoy some visits. You see, these days I have much to share, but no one who wants to hear it. I've bored Rachel from listening to my stories over and over again. She is such a saint!"

He laughed hard just in saying it.

She arrived right then carrying a tray, filling the room with the delicious aroma of coffee, accompanied by a fresh-baked cake.

My old pastor looked at her with a smile, in which I noticed more gratitude than words could convey, and she winked at him as if she still were a teenager.

I was spellbound as I witnessed that tender moment of love between those two lives that afternoon. I gathered that living in the shade of the cross preserves not only one's personal life but also one's marriage.

"So you have some stories to tell," I said to him after his wife had left the room.

"A lot," he told me. "And I think they're very good. Would you like to hear them?"

"It would be a pleasure," I said to him sincerely. I had a deep respect for my old pastor, and I felt myself growing just by being near him. How much more would I grow by listening to him?

For a moment I thought about telling him the dream I had had, which was the reason for this meeting, but I decided against it since I didn't want to influence the direction of our conversation.

"You know," he told me, "this morning I was remembering the exact time when I received my calling to serve God."

He lifted the coffee cup to his lips, but he stopped it just a few inches from his mouth, finishing his sentence: "I'm still moved just remembering it."

"How old were you?" I asked him.

"I'm not sure."

He took a sip of the steamy drink, placed the cup on the small plate, and lightly scratched his head, as if trying to stir his memory.

"Maybe when I was fifteen . . . I'm not sure. What I do remember perfectly is the powerful message that my pastor preached that day."

"So you liked it, then?"

"A lot, but it was something else that got my heart excited."

"Oh! And what was that?"

"The sure feeling that someday I would also be preaching that powerful message."

His eyes focused on the window, as if reading from the vast countryside the next part of his story.

"The end of that service was the beginning of my new life. I remained seated, with my head resting on the back of the seat in front of me, praying and crying—overwhelmed with emotion. Then I noticed a hand resting on my shoulder. It was my pastor's.

"'You've felt it, right?' he asked me warmly with an equally affirmative tone. 'You've felt your call. Haven't you?'

"I nodded my head yes, not knowing what else to say. I wanted to explain to him that such a calling seemed crazy to me. That God would choose me seemed like a mistake or a bad joke. Me, who was unable to even talk in front of three people, chosen by God to talk to a crowd?"

He made an attempt to laugh, then finished: "Mistake or a bad joke, I realized that I didn't have any other option."

He picked up the cup again and riveted his eyes on mine as he continued his story. "My pastor placed his hand on my chin, making me raise my gaze so he could talk to me eye to eye: 'If He is calling you, tell Him yes,' he said almost in a whisper." My old pastor was whispering now as he told the story. "'But I will never be able to serve Him,' I complained.

"'God does not call the equipped; rather, He equips those He calls. Do you understand?' my pastor told me, pointing to the cross that hung over the altar. 'It's all you need. Life doesn't start when you're twenty, or when you're forty. Life starts at Calvary. And that's where fruitful service begins as well. Let the cross be so present in you that it becomes your way of life and your rest.' It was a healing affirmation that would go with me the rest of my life."

His story complete, my old pastor quickly finished his coffee and placed the cup on its plate. And then he leaned back in his chair.

"When we talked on the phone the other day, you didn't give

me many details about the reason for your visit," he said, "but something tells me that you're facing the uncomfortable feelings that have plagued me my whole life."

"You too—?"

He didn't let me finish my question.

"Son."

I loved that he used that endearing term when he talked to me.

"From the time I could remember, I've always had the question: Will I help someone someday? Will I respond to such a high calling in a worthy manner?"

I found myself nodding in agreement. Even I couldn't have expressed my own feelings better.

"Yes," he went on. "I wasn't sure almost about anything, except that what I could do wouldn't help to change anybody's life. But then I discovered that this kind of questioning is crucial, because my doubts about my own competence forced me to draw near to God in search of resources, and there"—he pointed to some worn cushions that were lying on the floor—"is where my feelings are set in order. God's presence fills me inside with peace, and although I fall down undone at times, I always get up renewed."

The volume of his voice increased several levels.

"Transformed, victorious . . . and, most of all, renewed."

I could sense that his words were even renewing me.

"It's on our knees before Him where we find balance. When you're tempted to think you lack courage, look at the cross."

He stretched his hand toward the whole bookshelf, and I noticed that even the book stand was filled with that holy symbol, printed on the spines of the books, in pictures that hung on the wall, and in Bible verses written down.

"Look at the cross," he insisted. "That's how valuable you are to God."

I decided to be honest with my old pastor. "What's happening to me," I admitted, "is that I think that I lack the talent to fulfill the responsibilities that are expected of me. Anyone could do the same things that I do . . . and they would do them a lot better."

He watched me with a smile that conveyed understanding and empathy. "I'm remembering an old story. Would you like me to tell it to you?"

"Go right ahead," I told him.

He got comfortable in his chair, clasped his fingers together, and let his hands rest on his lap, and then he began:

The man entered the wise man's room very distressed. "I'm here, teacher," he said, "because I feel so numb that I don't have the desire to do anything. I'm told that I'm no longer useful, that I do everything wrong, that I'm clumsy and very dumb. How can I improve? What can I do so they value me more?"

Without looking at him, the teacher said to him, "I'm so sorry, son. I can't help you, since I have to solve my own problem first. Perhaps later . . ." He paused for a moment and then added, "If you want to help me, I could take care of this matter of mine, and then after that I could perhaps help you."

"Of . . . of course, teacher," the young man stuttered, feeling once again that he wasn't worth anything and his needs were always being put off.

"Well . . ." the teacher continued. He took off a ring he had on the little finger of his left hand and, giving it to the young man, said, "Take the horse that's outside there and ride to the market. I need to sell this ring because I have to pay a debt. You need to get the best price possible, and don't accept anything less than a gold coin. Go now, and return with a gold coin as fast as you can." The young man took the ring and left. As soon as he arrived at the market, he began to offer the ring to the merchants, who looked at it with interest until the young man said what he was asking for it.

When he mentioned the price of a gold coin, some laughed, others turned away, and only one old man was kind enough to take the time to explain to the young man that a gold coin was much too valuable to pay him in exchange for the ring. In an attempt to help, someone offered him a silver coin and a copper vessel, but the young man had instructions not to accept anything except a gold coin and to refuse any other offer. After offering the ring to everyone he came across in the market, over a hundred people, and feeling dejected by his failure, he mounted his horse and returned. How he wished he had a gold coin to give to his teacher and free him from his debt, so that he could finally receive his teacher's wisdom and help.

He entered the room and said, "Teacher, I'm sorry. I couldn't get the price you asked me to get. I might have been able to get two or three silver coins. But I don't think that I could have deceived anyone about the true value of the ring."

"What you've just said is very important, my young friend," the teacher said, smiling. "We first must know the true value of the ring. Go get back on your horse and go and see the jeweler. Who *would know better than him? Tell him that you want to sell the ring and ask him how much he'll give you for it. But no matter what he offers you, don't sell it to him. Return here with my ring."*

The young man got back on his horse and rode off again. The jeweler examined the ring in the light of his oil lamp. He looked at it with his magnifying glass, weighed it, and then told him, *"Tell your teacher, young man, that if he wants to sell it right now, I can't give him any more than fifty-eight gold coins for his ring."*

"Fifty-eight gold coins?" the young man exclaimed.

"Yes," replied the jeweler. *"I know that with some time, we could get about seventy coins, but if the sale is urgent . . ."*

The young man galloped back excitedly to his teacher's house to tell him what had just happened.

"Sit down," his teacher said after listening to him. *"You are like that ring: a unique and precious jewel. And as such, only an expert can determine your value. Why are you going through life hoping that someone will discover your true value?"*

As I pondered this story, my old pastor looked at me intensely. He pointed to the cross.

"He did it for you . . . That's how valuable you are to God. Trust the Expert," he said as he pointed upward. "His opinion is the only one that should matter to you. He knows what your true worth is."

I nodded in agreement, deciding to come prepared for my next visit with a notebook and pencil to take notes.

"It's true that sometimes God allows us to experience the bitter taste of apparent failure," he pointed out, "because many of our failures are more apparent than real. But even this is helpful, because that feeling forces us to grab hold of the compass of prayer and understand the enormous truth that only God exists, only God knows, only God is able."

"What a phrase!" I said, repeating it. "Only God exists, only God knows, only God is able."

Socrates summed it up very simply when they tried to credit him with gifted wisdom because they believed he deserved it. The Greek philosopher looked at the crowd that was applauding his wisdom, then pointed toward heaven and said, "Only God is the true wise One."

The day was coming to an end when I closed the blue door behind me.

The high cloud banks in the sky were orange, crisscrossed by even darker clouds, through which shone the purest blue.

Faraway barking reminded me that off in the distance life went on, although not as quiet or beautiful as this place, where the moon—the lady of the night—and the jasmine flowers began to stir up their cloying and warm aroma.

As I passed by the rosebush, a red flower caught my attention; it had bloomed among the white ones. I leaned over to smell it, surprised that the same stalk could produce flowers with such different colors. It had a distinct aroma, much more intense than its accompanying white ones.

I walked for a while through that empty countryside; it did not seem threatening to me but rather incredibly beautiful. It was completely silent, tainted only by the greeting of the first insects of the night.

I opened up my arms, raising them toward heaven, and the fading light behind me projected a cross in front of me, which my shadow had made.

The solitude seemed like heaven's waiting room to me.

I worshipped as I walked. First in silence, then with a whisper, but finally my heart exploded with a "Hallelujah!" that silenced even the insects.

Even the dog off in the distance stopped barking.

Tears and worship blended together until I finally arrived home.

"How did it go, dear?" my wife, Mary, asked, looking at me worried when she saw my red and swollen eyes.

I didn't say anything to her. I just hugged her for a long time. Then I pushed her away a little to look at her. Her beautiful countenance danced in my tears.

"Fine, my love," I said and hugged her again. "It went very well."

A little later, Mary, feeling much more peaceful, was resting. My calmness was now hers, and that night she slept with a peace she had not experienced lately because my anxiety had stolen it from her.

It would be morning for her soon. Her office opened at eight o'clock sharp.

I took a little longer to go to bed. I had a lot to think about.

Overcome with joy, I leaned out the window. The moon, round and a brilliant white, turned the night sky into a dome of light, and a perfumed mist rose from the garden below.

Only God exists, only God knows, only God is able . . . Only God is the true wise One.

I repeated it many times, until every one of my senses was filled with that powerful message.

I began to cry again from the amazing peace and happiness that flowed through me. And through my tears the light of the moon was reflected, taking on the shape of a brilliant cross laid out on an immense nocturnal canvas.

Night was deepening, and the temperature was falling.

Finally, something deep inside was beginning to wake up.

The Second Monday

Powerful Weakness

Just a glimpse of the glory of God will rip off all the medals from our chest, strip us of all titles, and knock us off our pedestals.

A ll week long I waited impatiently for the next Monday to arrive. I almost counted the hours that remained until I would meet with my old pastor again.

His welcome was as friendly as the last time, and I had hardly sat down across from him when he looked at me with a solemn intensity tinged with tenderness and began to speak, remembering with admirable precision all the details of our previous meeting.

"As I told you last Monday, you are extremely valuable, but you must keep yourself humble."

I realized that his goal was to maintain some balance in his counsel to me.

"While you are serving God, you will enjoy some triumphs. Remember, then, that success has a highly intoxicating component. Be careful that you do not get drunk from it."

That phrase made quite an impression on me, as if God's own chisel had carved it in me. I had to react quickly so as not to get caught up by it, for wisdom continued to flow out of the mouth of my old pastor.

"There are people who spend their strength on the foolish endeavor of becoming known, and, if possible, well known. What foolishness!"

There was no anger in his voice. He said it calmly, but the strength of his convictions was striking.

"I have never understood," he continued, "the endeavor to show off our abilities and values. Who are we trying to impress? Will our abilities cause God to stand with His mouth open? When He chooses a person, that person doesn't have to try hard to vindicate his talents; God will take care of that."

The strength with which he spoke was both contagious and refreshing.

"I have known enough ministers of the gospel infected by the virus of success to know that the smell of triumph acts like alcohol: it tends to go to our heads and befuddle us. It clouds our vision and makes us clumsy. That's why God allows obstacles to come our way and doesn't prevent us from making mistakes, because the resulting weakness can actually turn into our true strength."

His gaze emanated the glow of someone completely persuaded by the truth and who feels an urgency to share it.

"There is something even more difficult than overcoming failure."

I narrowed my eyes a bit suspiciously. *More difficult than overcoming failure?* I thought. For me, failing was equivalent to sinking down into a pit of depression.

"Something even more difficult than overcoming failure," he insisted, "is overcoming success."

He remained silent so that he could think on that, or perhaps to give me the option of replying. But then he suddenly continued, "The greatest enemies of your triumphs for tomorrow are your triumphs of today. It is well proven that for every hundred people who endure adversity, only one accepts prosperity. And I'm not referring only to economic prosperity. The medals, even those earned legitimately, can weigh so heavily on your chest that they turn into dead weight. Stripes, even those earned in honest conquests, can slump our shoulders down, nailing us to the ground."

He looked at me firmly again, while he said to me, "Get over your failures, but don't allow your triumphs to defeat you. At times victory can come by fleeing and real power in feeling weak."

"Have you ever felt weak?" I asked him.

"If you only knew . . ." He began to laugh. "If you could have seen inside me, you would have been surprised at the fear and trembling that overwhelmed me. Some days I had to tell myself a hundred times the words God spoke to the apostle Paul in 2 Corinthians 12:9: 'My strength is made perfect in weakness.'"

As I listened to that confession, I was calling to mind the many times I had seen that man boldly proclaim the message of the cross.

His words got through to us with a certainty from someone who knew very well what he was saying and why he was saying it.

He sat up a little in his chair and asked me if he could tell me another story. After telling him that I would love to listen to him, he began:

A long time ago in an ancient convent governed by a wise abbess, more than a hundred nuns used to pray, work, and serve God by living austere and quiet lives. One day, they were told that one of them would be sent to their province to preach the gospel. After long deliberation and consultation, it was decided to prepare Sister Clara, a young woman full of qualities, for the mission. They instructed her to study, so Clara spent many long years in the convent's library deciphering codexes and becoming proficient in their secret knowledge. When she had finished her studies, she knew the classics, she could read the Scriptures in their original languages, and she was an expert in medieval theological tradition. She preached in the convent, and everyone appreciated her skilled learning and the anointing of her words. When she finished her sermon, Sister Clara leaned over to the abbess and said, "May I go preach now?"

The old abbess looked at her as if she could read her thoughts and appreciated that Sister Clara had thousands of answers piled high in her mind. "Still not yet, daughter . . . not yet," she answered. She sent her then to the garden, where she worked from dawn to dusk, enduring the freezing cold of winter and the blistering heat of the summer. She pulled up stones and weeds, and took care of the stalks of the vineyard one by one. She learned to wait for the seeds to grow and to recognize by the rising of the sap when the time to prune the chestnuts had arrived. She gained another kind of wisdom, but it still was not enough.

The Mother Abbess then sent her to talk with the peasants. She listened to the clamor of their complaints because of their hard yoke of servitude. She heard rumors of uprisings and encouraged those who suffered from such injustice. The abbess called her, looked at her, and saw that her mind was full of answers and her eyes full of questions. "It's not time yet, my daughter. Go and pray."

Sister Clara spent a long time in the solitary hermitage on the mountain. When she returned, her soul had been transfigured. "Is it time yet?" she asked. No. The time still had not come.

An epidemic had been declared in the country, and Sister Clara was sent to take care of the afflicted. She stayed up many nights caring for the sick and cried bitterly from burying many of them. When the pestilence ended, she fell ill herself from exhaustion and sadness and was cared for by a family in the village. She learned to be weak and feel small; she allowed herself to be loved and so regained her peace. When she returned to the convent, the Mother Abbess looked at her, reading her soul, and found her more human and vulnerable. She had a serene look about her. Her mind was full of answers, her eyes full of questions, and her heart full of names.

"Now it's time, my daughter . . . Now, yes. Go and preach the gospel," she told her.[1]

The story moved me deeply.

My old pastor leaned toward me and summarized the story,

speaking very slowly. "All the wisdom and power of God would not have mattered much if she had not decided to become weak and surrender her life. Henry Miller said, 'If God is not love, it's not worth Him existing.'"

He shook his hand and continued, "The saying has its merits, but I believe it is right. There"—he pointed to one of the numerous crosses that decorated his office—"are no miracles, no learning . . . just a broken body from which love drains out on all four sides. In that extreme weakness victory was forged. That is how it is, and there is no other way. Son, if we want to be effective, we have to imitate Him. God is not looking for celebrities, nor does He choose His servants consulting celebrity magazines; He prefers vessels of clay to administer His treasure, and the sooner we come to terms that our calling is not about becoming statues but rather platforms, the sooner we will advance."

I listened to his profound counsel.

"Self-sufficiency is a highly sought-after quality on earth, but it's a real hindrance in the things of the kingdom. God helps us until we feel powerful, but it's in our self-sufficiency that our downfall begins. Fewer things exert such influence as humility that is established at the altar. But it is an abomination to turn the altar into a stage."

He was quiet for a moment before confirming it.

"Some churches have converted their altars into stages," he denounced, "and that is a real problem. On a stage is where celebrities shine; on an altar is where God's presence comes down. The two are incompatible; we will have to choose: human celebrities or godly impact."

My old pastor was shaking his head, moving his chin almost from shoulder to shoulder, in a flat denial and a firm conviction. "It is a terrible absurdity, listening to the simple message of the gospel preached by arrogant lips.

"Don't forget it," he said as he returned to the heart of the teaching he wanted to convey to me.

"Humility is not an option but a nonnegotiable requirement for whoever serves God. Prayer will help us as well."

He pointed to the cushions on the floor again, and this time I noticed they were marked with cracks made by his knees.

"Prayer lifts our spirits up, but at the same time, it keeps our feet on the ground."

He wanted to make this point very clear, so he added, "I'm referring to genuine spirituality, not playing at mysticism. I have seen students of prayer who believe they are more spiritual than the rest. They're like mystical saints who 'levitate' and look down with pride at others, and even dare to judge them." He leaned toward me as one who was going to say something in confidence and said, "I firmly believe that there is no worse arrogance than spiritual pride; it is the kind that stinks the most. Do you know what happens with pride? It's like bad breath. Everyone notices it except the person who has it."

His laughter ended his joke, and it was delightful to me.

"Those 'fans' of prayer who become arrogant hardly even gaze into the realm of God's fellowship, and they already feel superior to the rest of us mortals. Pride is like a hairpin that pierces the skull and hardens and blocks the neurons. How different are those who decide to shelter themselves completely in the heart of God! They come forth filled with life and also with humility. Just a glimpse of His glory will suddenly tear all the medals from our chests, strip us of our titles, and knock us off our pedestals. Whoever rides on the shoulders of pride, brandishing the sword of judgment and spewing forth opinions on everything and everyone, still has not come face-to-face with the majesty of God. Because whoever approaches the Lord's throne is instantly cured of the desire for fame. Closeness to God simplifies everything."

My old pastor closed his eyes, and I assumed that he was peering into that unique realm of prayer. Then I realized he had not spent his best moments sitting in that sofa, but rather kneeling on those worn-out cushions, because his best view was not the one that the large window in his office offered. Instead, the more sublime scenery was the one he contemplated while kneeling, gazing at the immense meadows of heaven.

I closed my eyes, too, convinced that for today, that was enough.

I did not have a single question for him, but I took away a thousand answers. I had discovered a simple and yet transforming key: only God is able, only God knows, and only God serves. And His power is seen in vessels of clay . . . in simple instruments . . . in humble servants.

My old pastor must have opened his eyes and seen mine closed, because I heard his voice, deep and profound, rising up in prayer. He said many things about me to God, so many and so right-on that I began to think that this venerable old man had been running beside me on the last leg of the journey. It was more than that. I understood the real possibility that he had plumbed the depths of me, understanding every one of my feelings, because as he spoke to God, he described in detail the sleeplessness of my last few nights and the doubts of my last few days. He spoke to God about my present and future uncertainty.

And as he prayed, God listened.

I know He was listening, because a different kind of air filled me inside. It was as if I was breathing brand-new oxygen—pure, revitalizing strength.

Night was falling when I left his house.

The blue door had closed, but I hesitated a moment, delighting myself in the mild night temperature.

My eyes took in the small garden. The silhouette of the trees cut off their own shadows in the darkness as their branches swayed to the rhythm of the mild gusts of warm wind.

Just as I was about to begin walking away, I noticed the rose-bush. My curiosity made me look for the red flower from last Monday, and I was surprised to see another one beginning to open.

A second red rose on that white rosebush.

When I arrived home, I went to my office and searched in the closet until I came across something I had neglected for weeks: a worn-out cushion that in times past I had knelt on daily. I placed it on the floor, and then I sunk on my knees on top of the forgotten cushion. I closed my eyes and felt heaven open.

There was no doubt that He was there, and He was smiling at me.

Leaning my head on His chest, I felt a real peace, almost tangible, that dripped through my senses until it settled in my soul.

The Third Monday

Servant of God or Church Executive?

God is not as interested in our productivity as much as He is in our life. He loves fellowship much more than production.

The beautiful feeling lasted for several days, but halfway through the week, it began to dissipate, giving place to other feelings a lot less pleasant.

My days flowed on almost all the same: Mary left early for her office, and I went to my office.

Daybreak would find me sitting at the table, and the sun rays would converge on my open daily planner, casting light on the multiple obligations that were crowded together there. The reading of a psalm and a routine prayer, more out of trying to calm my conscience than to connect with God, were the only vestiges of spirituality that would fill the day.

But it hadn't always been that way.

27

Awhile back, prayer was my greatest claim. Early morning was always my favorite time, and the first light of day would find me kneeling and immersed in my delight: talking to God and letting Him talk to me.

Lately, however, too many obligations had displaced that intimate pleasure. My times of prayer were now filled with organizing, and the search for inspiration yielded its time to planning. The funny thing is that it all had to do with God's work, but not so much with the God of the work. I was so busy serving Him that I didn't have any time to talk with Him.

I kept on "cooking" for God, but I had kicked God out of the kitchen.

Without realizing it, I had stopped being God's servant and turned myself into a church executive—a very busy executive with an open agenda and a closed Bible.

There was a time when serving was a privilege . . . not today. Now I finished many of my workdays not only tired but unsatisfied and more and more disappointed.

Mary noticed it and longed for the arrival of the following Monday more than I did.

"Will you come back next Monday?" my old pastor had asked me as we said good-bye.

"May I?" I had asked longingly. "You don't mind if I come back?"

"I implore you to." He had emphasized his words with the pressure of his hand on my shoulder.

The next Monday, I stopped in front of the blue door with the expectation of a sick person about to cross the threshold of a hospital, longing to find a cure.

"Welcome!"

The ever-present smile on Rachel's face appeared to have been painted by a hand that, in capturing it, had filled it with complete joy. Her eyes smiled. It seemed that instead of being there for sight, her eyes were there to light up her face, gracing her with a confident look that was totally trustworthy. "Come in," she said to me. "It's hot outside."

"How are the two of you doing?" I said, asking indirectly about my old pastor.

Not seeing him seemed strange to me.

"Well . . ." A slight shadow seemed to dim the glow of her face, but it soon came back. "These last days, he has been a little gloomy, but it doesn't appear to be anything serious."

"I wouldn't want to be a bother." I stopped and did not enter. "If he isn't doing well, I can come back another day."

"No, please," she said to me, grabbing my arm. "Your visit will be good for him. Come in. He is in his room."

She went ahead, leading the way toward his room.

A picture with striking color caught my attention, one I had not noticed the previous day.

"What is this?" I dared to ask.

Rachel took it down. "It's a fable that my husband loves," she said, laughing. "You already know how fond he is of stories."

"May I read it?"

"Of course!" she said, handing it to me.

The text was written in white letters over a background that was the color of the sky:

*A tourist who was visiting a small village approached the house
of a well-known wise man, and he was surprised to see that he*

lived in a small, humble room filled with books. The only pieces of
furniture were a bed, a table, and a chair.

"Where is the rest of your furniture?" the tourist asked.

"And where is yours?" the wise man answered back.

"Mine?" responded the tourist, surprised. "I'm only here for
a short time."

"Me too," said the wise man.

"It's a great truth," I said as I gave the picture back to Rachel.

"And the motto of our life," she added. "We have always tried
not to have too much dead weight. You already know that owning
only a few things makes it easier to leave."

"That's true," I agreed. "To lift off and take flight, it's necessary to have as little baggage as possible. Too many possessions
can weigh down someone who wants to rise up and visit the
heights. Henry Van Dyke said something similar: 'Happiness is
something on the inside, not on the outside; therefore, it doesn't
depend on what we have, but rather who we are.'"

She looked at me thoughtfully, with a friendliness that I felt
was sincere. She smiled again and said, "You and my husband
have been talking about the cross, isn't that right?"

"Yes, we have."

"Have you stopped to think about how many things are contained in the cross?"

I thought about that for a moment, and then I answered, "As
your husband told me the other day, 'Him . . . only Him . . . no
one else but Him.'"

"And yet," she declared, "there is no greater treasure than

that contained within the cross. There are few things that are really necessary to live abundantly! Don't you agree? I believe it was Benjamin Franklin who said that happiness is not achieved by great strokes of luck that only can happen occasionally, but rather by small things that happen every day."

"That's right," I admitted. "Like the words of Leo Tolstoy when he realized, "'My happiness consists in the fact that I know how to appreciate what I have, and I don't greatly desire what I don't have.'"

"A good thought," Rachel said as she returned the picture to the wall.

Then she walked forward and opened the door to the office.

My old pastor was praying, with his knees perfectly fit into the marks on the cushions. At the sound of the door, he turned around.

"Oh!" He stood up with effort and flushed somewhat.

He almost blushed, taking on a timid and delightful childish expression, as if he had been caught doing something wrong. "Forgive me, I didn't realize it was time for your visit. I didn't even hear you arrive."

"Nothing to worry about," I told him as I approached to give him a hug. "You were engaged in a worthy activity. How are you?"

I kept my hand on his shoulder, for he seemed a bit downhearted. "Rachel tells me that you've not been feeling well these last few days."

"It's nothing," he smiled. "You know how it is. It's just the aches and pains of old age."

"I'll bring you both some coffee," Rachel said as she headed for the kitchen.

"I would prefer tea," he said. "Chamomile tea, please."

He sat down in his chair and gestured with his hand for me to do the same.

"And so?" He leaned forward and patted my knee. "How did your week go?"

"Last Monday I left this house renewed," I answered. "It was incredible how I was able to appropriate the truths you had taught me, but by Wednesday the feeling had faded . . . I suppose from hurried and urgent matters."

After a long, thoughtful pause, he looked at me with a somewhat solemn expression, and his voice broke the deep well of silence that had opened up between us.

"The issue is that last Monday you took a small bite, but you have to feed yourself every day, refilling your reservoir and renewing yourself."

"How can I do that?"

"I don't know of a better fountain of resources than communion with God," he said with conviction. "Every minute in His presence recharges our batteries and makes us stronger."

"It's not easy," I confessed. "There are so many things to take care of that I can't get everything done."

I thought of Mary . . . and the little time I spent with her and the abandonment I had subjected her to at times.

"There are too many fronts to cover. If you saw my agenda . . ."

My old pastor preferred to ignore my biased self-importance that, almost unconsciously, I had displayed in my comment, and he nodded with understanding.

"I don't quite understand why I can't seem to get my friend Philip out of my mind today," he said.

"Philip?"

Except for Jesus' disciple, I didn't remember knowing anyone who had that name, and even given how old my old pastor was, that didn't make him a contemporary of the apostle.

"We graduated from the same Bible school," he explained, "although he excelled much more than me, and his career took off instantly. He was an incredible guy, a real combination of anointed abilities with authentic charisma. He climbed the ladder with unstoppable ease, almost as if he had been predestined for the top, which in the end he achieved. He dedicated his best years to forming a prosperous church and speaking about the spiritual life in large conventions all over the world."

The old man paused, forced by sadness, I thought. Then he continued, "Little by little he began to lose contact with his family. His wife became indifferent and reserved. Believing that God and the church had stolen her husband from her, she felt very offended. One day my friend Philip got involved in an affair with his young secretary, which was as passionate as it was regrettable. When I confronted him, he said to me sadly, 'The work I did for God has worn me out. The overload of all the work has left me weak and almost defenseless. When the temptation presented itself, I didn't have the strength to resist. I couldn't believe what I had done. I couldn't believe that I had become involved with another woman . . . I believe the ministry had turned into just a business, and God was very distant.'"

My old pastor had closed his eyes, and his demeanor

reflected a wince of pain. My reaction was one of astonishment. Nevertheless, he went on with his story: "When his wife found out about the affair, she left him. He regretted what he had done in tears: 'I would give anything to turn the clock back. I focused all my energy on achieving success in the ministry, and I neglected my relationship with God, whom I was serving, and my family, who should have been working alongside me in that work.'"

I kept quiet. The story was overwhelming and painfully instructive. I didn't even realize that he was staring at me until I heard him ask, "How much time do you spend in prayer?"

The question was direct, almost impertinent. I must confess it made me feel very uncomfortable.

"Well..."

I did not want to lie to him, but the reality of how things really were was hard and somewhat embarrassing. "I do what I can," I said.

He knew exactly how to interpret my camouflaged answer and understand that my prayer life was suffering. Perhaps it already was just a dead body.

"Nothing," and he repeated it with a maddening slowness, accentuating every syllable, "absolutely nothing is as important as taking time to be with God. It's that time that keeps us soft-hearted. It prepares us, tunes us, and conditions the growth in our lives."

His emphatic sentences, charged with logic, put me on the defensive.

"I would love to have time to pray." I was sincere in what I was saying to him. "But there are many fronts to cover."

There once was a woodcutter who showed up at a log mill . . .

My old pastor was launching into one of his stories without warning, so I prepared myself to listen attentively.

. . . The pay was good, and the working conditions were, too, so the woodcutter decided to be a good example. The first day he introduced himself to the foreman, who gave him an ax and assigned him to a certain spot in the forest. The man was excited and went out into the forest to work, and in one single day he cut down eighteen trees.

"Congratulations," the foreman told him. "Keep it up."

Encouraged by the foreman's words, the woodcutter decided to improve on his work the next day. So he went to bed early that night, and the next morning he got up very early, before anyone else, and went out into the forest. He worked very hard, but he was only able to cut down fifteen trees. "I must be very tired," he said, so he decided to go to bed at sundown. When dawn came, he decided to beat his record of eighteen trees. However, that day he wasn't able to even cut down half that number. The next day he only cut down seven, then five, and the last day he spent all afternoon trying to cut down his second tree. Worried about what his foreman would say, the woodcutter went to tell him what was happening and to promise that he was giving it his best. The foreman asked him: "When was the last time you sharpened your ax?"

"Sharpen my ax? I haven't had time. I was too busy cutting down trees."

He was quiet for a short time, then he went on to finish:

When the ax gets dull, we will have to spend double the energy to obtain half the results.[1]

He spoke with a mixture of determination and gentleness that filled every single one of his words with conviction.

"Sometimes the wisest thing to do is to stop, interrupt the felling of trees, and sharpen the ax. That way, half the energy will then double the results. Prayer, talking with God and having intimate communion with Him, is the way our axes get sharpened again."

"Are you asking me to abandon my responsibilities to spend my whole day knelt down in prayer?" Even I was surprised by the insolence with which I questioned him.

"Not at all." He said it with determination but without a hint of hardness. "It has nothing to do with neglecting our responsibilities, but rather soaking them in prayer."

He leaned back and closed his eyes for a moment, then without opening them, he went on: "We can work without praying, or we can do it while we pray, soaking every place, every appointment, and every activity with God's presence. That turns work into serving and transforms our activity into something effective."

He opened his eyes and put his hand on my shoulder to make sure I was paying attention.

"Serve as you pray and pray as you serve. What may seem to be *outward* prayer inactivity actually releases a powerful action. Minutes spent with God produce great gains for every second of our lives. Focus your attention first and foremost on God rather than on men. That way when you stand before them you will have treasures to share, and those are what are worthwhile, son."

Once again he used the endearing term that I had come to like so much.

"The riches taken from the heart of God, the sentences we hear from His mouth, the works that He shares with us in that intimate place . . . those are what give life and make a difference."

"Okay, that makes sense," I realized. "It means allowing God to enter into every activity I undertake. Talking to Him and entrusting myself to His grace every moment."

My old pastor looked at me intently.

"Too often," he went on, "we who serve God often confuse success with victory. We try to attain great achievements, and we forget that God loves us for who we are, not for what we do. If the church you are pastoring right now were to grow and become the largest one in the world, God wouldn't love you any more than He already does . . . but if that church were to close because of lack of attendance, He wouldn't love you any less. By focusing on success, we confuse it with victory. Christ did not live obsessed with drawing crowds, but when He had them, He confronted them in such a way that many of them went away. The cross? There were a handful of people gathered around the foot of it, but we don't highly esteem signs of success regarding it; nevertheless, the cross was the greatest victory that anyone has ever achieved. *Success* is a term from the business world. *Victory* is a term used for combat."

He leaned forward toward me as usual to make sure he had my complete attention.

"We are not involved in a business, but rather a war. And God loves His soldiers much more than the results."

He had my complete attention, and he must have noticed my desire to continue listening because he added, "I will tell you a story."

He set his Bible on the small table beside his chair and began:

Once upon a time near a river there was a tree that loved a little boy very much. The little boy would often go and visit the tree: he would climb up the trunk, swing from the branches, eat its fruit, and then rest in its shade. After a long relationship of friendship, the little boy moved away, leaving the tree alone for a long time. Until one day— one good day—the tree looked off in the distance and saw the figure of the young boy approaching. Filled to the brim with happiness, the tree said to him, "Come here, my friend, climb up my trunk, swing in my branches, eat my fruit, rest in my shade; stay with me."

The little boy, who had now grown into an adolescent, said to the tree, "I'm not a little boy who just plays now. I've grown up now, and I need money to buy a lot of things."

"I'm sorry," the tree answered sadly. "I don't have any money, but if you would like to, you can climb through my branches and pick my fruit. You could take it to the market and sell it. That way you could get money to buy what you want." The young boy didn't even let the tree repeat it a second time. He climbed up into the tree and picked all the fruit. Almost bent over from all the weight of it, he disappeared off in the horizon and was not seen again.

The tree remained all alone for a long time. Several years later he saw his old friend approaching, and he now was a man.

Filled with happiness, the tree welcomed him: "Come here, my friend. Play with me as you used to do. Hoist yourself up my trunk, swing in my branches . . . stay with me."

"No," answered the man. "I'm too busy to play. Now I want to marry and have children, but I need to build a house where I can live."

"I'm sorry," said the tree, "I don't have a house for you. My house is the forest. But if you want to, you can climb my trunk and cut off my branches. With those you would be able to build a house where you could live with your family." The tree didn't even have to wait for answer. Soon the man disappeared off on the horizon dragging behind him a mountain of branches, and he was not seen again. Once again, the tree remained alone.

Many years later, he spotted the figure of a man off in the distance, and he recognized his old friend. Once again he was filled with joy.

"Have you come to stay this time? Rest in my shade. Stay with me."

"No," said the man. "I feel very alone, and I want to travel to a far-off country to meet new people. But I don't have a way to get there."

"I'm sorry that you're not happy," the tree said to the man. "I'm not sure how to help you, because there isn't much left of me, but if you want to, you may cut my trunk and make it into a canoe. A river flows nearby that that could carry you to the land where you could find happiness." The man could hardly believe he had found a solution for his dream. So he set about to work and built a canoe and set off on his journey.

The tree stump that was left remained alone for many long years. Until one fine day the tree stump saw an old man slowly approaching in the distance. When the old man was closer, the tree stump could still see in his face some vestiges of the little boy from so many years ago. With sadness in his voice, the small tree stump whispered, "I'm sorry, my friend, but I don't have anything to give you. I don't have fruit to feed you, nor a trunk you can climb up in, nor branches for you to swing on."

"I appreciate that," answered the old man, "but I don't need anything anymore. I'm only looking for a place to sit down and rest."

"In that case," the tree stump answered happily, "sit down on me and rest."

And the old man finally stayed with the tree and found rest.[2]

"Did you like that one?" my old pastor asked me.

"To be honest, I didn't like the individual in the story."

"Do you think he deserved what the tree gave him?"

"Absolutely not," I answered resolutely.

"That is grace," he stated. "An unmerited gift. The essence of the story is that God longs to have fellowship with us. Our emphasis is to 'do things for God,' but He doesn't love us for what we do for Him but rather for who we are. God is not focused on our productivity but rather our life. He loves fellowship much more than production. He prefers to have friends over servants. God is more pleased to look on clean hands rather than full hands. Do you remember the words of Jesus in John 15:15? 'No longer do I call you servants . . . but I have called you friends.' A time of swinging in His branches or sitting in His shade is miraculous for us and delightful for Him. Too often we perceive God as a demanding boss looking for results, but He is a loving Father. In fact, He is such a loving Father that He enjoys romping on the floor with His children and laughing with them until His stomach hurts. That's incomprehensible but possible."

He became silent for a moment, then he turned his face toward me.

"We can be as close to God as Jesus' mother Mary, who watched God work, sweat, eat, laugh, or cry; smelling Him, touching the calluses of His carpenter hands, and knowing that He was the Messiah. The great *kyrios*, Lord of lords. Don't you doubt it for a moment. God loves fellowship much more than work."

"Where did the tree get the strength to keep giving over and over again?" I asked, not able to shake off my feeling of antipathy toward that man and feeling compassion for the tree.

"The man coveted the tree's benefits," he told me, "but the tree longed for the man's companionship; and in order to gain fellowship, he gave the man everything."

"That is love!" I concluded.

"Grace is love in action," he declared. "The tree loved, and that is why he gave not only what he had but what he was. He gave himself. It's possible to give without loving, but it's totally impossible to love without giving—"

"And finally," I interrupted, "the lonely man found rest sitting on that tree."

"Exactly! And that is also the message of the cross," declared my old pastor. "We can come to it looking for benefits, but the true benefit is not in visiting it, but remaining there."

Right then, Rachel entered the office with coffee. "How's the afternoon going?" she asked. "Have you had a constructive conversation?"

"Well," the old pastor answered, "I am boring our friend with my stories."

"No, not at all," I answered. "I love listening to him."

"You really love it?" Rachel laughed. "Well, then, you'll just have to listen to me now."

So Rachel sat down, ready to begin her story. I got comfortable in my chair, ready to enjoy it.

A wise Greek man was exploring the land. He felt satisfied and proud of his knowledge of philosophy and science. On one occasion he had to cross a river, so he boarded a boat. The old boatman rhythmically rowed the oars and looked distractedly at the water. Then the wise man asked him, "Do you know astronomy?"

"No, sir."

"Well, then, you've lost a fourth of your life. Do you know philosophy?"

"No, sir."

"Well, then, you've lost a fourth of your life. You must at least know ancient history."

"No, sir."

"Well, then, you've lost another fourth of your life."

Right then, a blast of wind violently shook the boat and tipped it over. Both men fell into the water. The boatman effort-lessly swam toward the riverbank. Once there, he observed the

wise man desperately waving his hands in the water. The river
was quite swollen, and the current was strong.

"Do you know how to swim, my wise friend?"

"No!" he shouted in desperation. "I don't know how to swim!"

"Well, then, you've lost all of your life."[3]

"That is a brilliant story," I applauded.

"And it contains an enormous truth," Rachel explained, feeling complimented. "Human beings live worried about a lot of things, but only a few things are really necessary."

When I left the house, a gentle breeze stirred my hair and caused the highest branches in the trees to sway. The long stems of the rosebush were also swaying, one of which displayed the first fresh healthy red roses, alongside a new flower that was beginning to open, barely showing its deep red petals.

I gently touched them as I whispered, "Grace is receiving that which we do not deserve; mercy is not receiving what we do deserve."

I set out toward home pondering the reflections that my old pastor had pointed out from Rachel's story.

"You're right," I had told him, "that there are very few things that truly are essential. The sad thing is that those few things are not the priority of most people."

I wanted to ask him, *What are those few things?* but I already knew the answer.

"One thing is needed, and Mary has chosen that good part." My old pastor had quoted the scene with Martha and Mary that is found in Luke 10:42.

"To sit at the feet of Jesus," I had ventured, "that is the number one priority, right?"

He had nodded in agreement and then finished, "To contemplate Him . . . listen to Him . . . That is true delight."

That was my old pastor's great success, his wise choice, and the reason that this man and his wife exuded genuine life from every pore of their skin.

Hardly realizing it, I walked back again to the blue door and gazed at the rosebush. Never had I seen such hardy stems that produced such unique roses. I was convinced that those flowers had a message, but I did not want to hasten the solving of the enigma.

There was a new moon that plunged everything into almost total darkness, but the shadows from below only made the lights above all that much larger, allowing me to see the heavens adorned with thousands of stars in ecstatic beauty. Each brilliant light in the firmament seemed like a gem by which God was declaring His love for me.

"The key"—my old pastor had said to me when we said goodbye—"is not in what you serve, but rather whom you serve. You have two options: serve the Lord or work in the church. They are not the same"—he shook his head back and forth adamantly—"not even similar. Don't work *for* God, work *with* God. And that intimacy"—he had closed his eyes as if tasting it right then with delight—"will renew and encourage you in an extraordinary way. Working *for* God will turn you into an employee of the church, but serving *with* God will make you a collaborator with Him whom you love. You will be in love with Him and will not want to even think about living for someone else or giving yourself to some other cause. In that moment you will not only be more active but you will be more effective."

I returned home walking very slowly, but with a heart beating faster. I thought about God and discovered that I did love Him. Then I thought about serving Him, and the fearful trembling of days past did not grab hold of me.

The feeling I had now was very similar to that of the time of my first love.

I closed my eyes and worshipped. I thought about the cross, the symbol of His love.

I felt free and forgiven. For one eternal second, I experienced pure happiness that seemed to never end.

I immediately began to laugh and cry like one who was in love.

The Fourth Monday

The Biggest Disappointment

Love them. Even those who despise you . . . especially them,
because those who deserve it the least are the ones who need
it the most.

The week was marked by putting into practice the advice
from my old pastor, and amazingly it worked.

The cushion I used to recline on as a *prie-dieu*, a prayer stool,
did not return to the closet. Instead, it remained on the floor next
to my chair.

After Mary would leave for the office, I would kneel on the
cushion until it was time for me to go to work. There, down on my
knees, I felt that my feelings as well as my day were put in order.

That time was not characterized by supernatural experiences, trembling, or shivers. It was a sacred time that brought
clarity to everything and set the tone for every day.

That Wednesday Mary could not help notice it: "Sweetheart," she said to me, "I see a change in you. You're much calmer and happier."

I took her in my arms and kissed her tenderly. Drawing closer to God had renewed my love for Him, and that affected all the rest of my relationships: I was treating my wife differently, and, in general, I had a much improved outlook on life. I discovered that living in love with God was like standing high up in a lookout that provides a different perspective on everything and everyone.

Unfortunately, life not only has bright spots but also shadows, and the best moment in the life of a person, of any person, can often sadly end up short-lived. Who—if they were able to—wouldn't want to copy it, multiply it, and make it last forever?

That would have been my desire with the feelings that overwhelmed me that whole week, and I would have returned the next Monday exultant if it hadn't been for the terrible disappointment I suffered that Friday.

The telephone rang while we were eating dinner that day, so my wife went to answer it.

A short while later she returned.

It was late afternoon, but suddenly a total darkness came over us. Mary had turned pale as she stood there holding the cordless telephone. Her appearance startled me. She was as white as wax, and her facial expression indicated true anguish.

I was worried, so I took the phone from her and identified myself. The voice that answered on the other end was dripping with bitterness.

It was a close friend in whom lately we had noticed something strange. And now, without even taking the time to say hello, he proceeded to dump all his indignation over the phone line, choosing to do it with the most wounding and insulting words. He had done it first to my wife, which left her in a miserable state, and now he was going off on me, forcing me to listen to a stream of unjust accusations that were summed up in: "You will never preach the word again to me or to my family."

After he had finished going off on me, he hung up without giving me the option of replying. I was thunderstruck.

I stared at the cordless phone that had just been the conduit through which poisonous darts had been hurled at my soul, and the worst of it was they had been hurled at my wife as well.

I looked at her.

Mary's face was a grimace of astonishment. In her eyes, which were fixed on mine, I could read many questions: *"Why?" "Why did he offend us?" "Why is he accusing us? "Why is he insulting us?" "Why?" "Why?" "Why?"*

Mary let herself fall onto the chair, and I hung up the phone. I sat down in front of her. She had buried her face in her hands and was crying.

With all my strength I wanted to convey words of encouragement, but no words came to mind. I went from indignation to discouragement, and suddenly I felt very tired. Depressed, I stared at the floor. Mary continued to cry.

The food on the table was getting cold.

Then my eyes saw the cross that was the focal point in the living room of our home, an empty cross . . . but one filled with messages. At that moment, the solitary cross began to speak to me of the revilements suffered by the One who had hung there.

Injustice would be the word that defines the reason that the praetorians had crucified Him. The treatment He received and each blow that was laid on Him was unjust. The hammer blows on the nails that pierced His body were unjust. The insults and spitting . . . it all was unjust.

Even the message that sprang from the lips of the One who was being executed unfairly was unjust: *Forgive them . . .*

Justice would have been to strike them all dead. But that story was not about justice; it was about mercy.

Forgive them . . . I meditated on that and it stirred me. *Forgive them . . . forgive them . . .*

Suddenly, I found myself hugging my wife and whispering in her ear: "Forgive them . . . forgive them . . . forgive them . . ."

My moist cheek was right up next to hers, which also was drenched, and my eyes remained fixed on the cross as my heart took in the message: *Forgive them . . .* The words, repeated a thousand times, infused peace into my soul.

Forgive them.

Yet I have to confess that I hardly slept that night. As soon as I closed my eyes, the telephone episode resurfaced, stubbornly raising its head out from the edge of my memory. The echo of the insults reverberated in my mind with such intensity that it stunned me.

The night was long and difficult, and my mind escaped uncontrollably upward toward black heavens filled with rebukes and bitterness. I tried hard to bring my mind back to earth, returning it to the land of forgiveness . . . I tried hard, but I was not able to do it.

Tired of turning over and over, I got up long before dawn. As I wet my eyes, swollen from lack of sleep, I looked at myself in the mirror and saw that somewhere in my soul had risen a wall of resentment.

I realized that I wouldn't be able to serve with resentment, and so I thought it would be better to stop serving.

And then the anguish really began to tear me up inside.

The visit to my old pastor shone like a lighthouse amid enormous waves in a turbulent sea as I dragged my battered ship toward the blue door of that refuge.

"Hello! Please come in. He's resting," Rachel told me with a look filled with apology. "Would you like something to drink while he wakes up?"

I noticed a touch of sadness in her eyes, which was unusual, as was the fact that my old pastor was sleeping at this hour.

"No thank you, Rachel," I said as I pointed toward the well-cared-for garden. "I'll just walk around here for a while. The garden is charming. Are you the one who takes care of it?"

"I do what I can," she said modestly. "The plants are appreciative, and the garden is small. It isn't much work to keep it up."

We spent a fair amount of time walking through it while she explained the characteristics and details of every one of the plants.

"Well," she finally said to me, "I believe it's time to wake him up. If not, he'll never sleep tonight."

I followed her, and as we walked through the living room, a journal much larger than a normal-sized one, which was lying open on the table, caught my attention. In a burst of boldness, I asked her, "What is this?"

"It's his prayer journal," she answered me, then laughed as she added, "a very special prayer journal. It contains a list of those persons who have offended us the most over the course of our ministry, and we pray for every one almost every day. My husband always says that those who hurt us the most are the ones who need God the most. That's why we pray for them twice as much. Besides, he says that if he prays for those who offend us it's impossible for him to hold evil feelings against them. When we pray, he always tells me, 'Resentment that wants to sprout forth dies before it is born, and in its place arises a sweet and forgiving love.'"

I looked at that journal with fascination as the image of my wife, collapsed in the chair with her face buried in her hands, teetered on the surface of my conscience.

Rachel added, "Rest assured that it cost me dearly to admit that about praying for those who had hurt us, but when I was finally able to do it, I realized that it worked—"

"Well, I'll be!"

The voice of my old pastor startled both of us, causing us to turn our heads.

"So you're talking about my prayer journal."

"Hello!" I said to him as I hugged him. I noticed he looked disheartened. "Forgive my boldness. I saw this journal, and I asked Rachel what it was. It certainly has impressed me to discover your keeping a prayer record of all those who have wounded the two of you."

"Does that surprise you?" he said in a tone more serious than normal. "I soon realized that the day I stopped loving them I would have to stop serving them." He was emphatic. "It is impossible to serve those you don't love with a right spirit. Ministering to them with resentment will destroy them."

He stopped, but only for a moment. Then to stress his point, he emphasized each word as he shook his index finger: "Words that are spoken based on wounds are venomous arrows, and actions carried out from resentment are poison darts."

I opened the journal and let the pages flip through my fingers. There were dozens of written pages. Endless names had been added to the list over the years. Names of offenders who, in exchange for their harm, had received blessings.

The serious tone of the old man startled me: "They will hurt you. Don't doubt that, and they will hurt the ones you love, but when that happens, do not pour out your indignation on people. Draw near to God, speak to Him about it, and fill yourself up with that same feeling that made Jesus love those who attacked, humiliated, and finally killed Him. Look at the cross. No one has ever loved like God, and no one has ever been hated as much as He."

For a few seconds, I continued to meditate on his words: *They will hurt you . . . they will hurt the ones you love . . . do not pour out your indignation on people. . . . Look at the cross. No one has ever loved like God, and no one has ever been hated as much as He.*

"I'm not God."

My insolent answer could only have been a result of how sensitive I was because of what I had gone through that week. To ease the tension, I added, "I find it very difficult to love those who hurt us so unjustly."

He looked at me, somewhat surprised by my vehement reaction, and smiled before asking me: "Something has happened, hasn't it?"

I lowered my head, and with my gaze fixed on the floor, I explained, "This week my wife and I were treated very unjustly. I was very disheartened, and Mary is still in pretty bad shape."

Rachel, who was very wise, excused herself, saying she had to tend to some obligations, while my old pastor put his hand on my shoulder and pointed the way to his office.

"Look," he said as he sat in his chair, and I sat in front of him. "Serving others means opening your heart and loving; that makes us vulnerable. The more you love, the more you make yourself vulnerable, because to love means making our heart a bull's-eye for those we love. And loving also means forgiving."

Those words contained enormous truths, but what loomed even bigger to me was the disappointment I had stuffed inside. Together with the feelings of the last few weeks, it had me just about derailed.

"I haven't rested well the last few nights," I told him. Then I added, "When I'm wide-awake I'm harassed by terrible thoughts. In fact, I've had the time to think about it, and I decided that it's not worth continuing to pastor my church. I don't believe that I love them, and they don't love me either. I'm hurting my wife by blindly fulfilling some functions that I'm not qualified for . . . responsibilities I probably wasn't even called to. I'm carrying out a job that someone else could fulfill a lot better than me. I just want to be right with God, right with people, and right with my wife. I only want everything to be all right!" I repeated louder than necessary. "And it's not working."

Like an echo to the storm in my soul, a sudden strong wind stirred up in the garden. The trees shook, and the enormous oak tree, shaken by successive gusts of wind, shed a heavy shower of leaves.

"Poor Rachel," my old pastor said sadly as he gazed at the ground where the leaves whirled together by the wind. "She spent all yesterday afternoon sweeping the garden, and now look at how it has become in just a few seconds."

"I am so sorry," I answered with little concern, surprised that something so trivial would take precedence over my huge problem.

"Would you be so kind as to sweep up this little mess?"

I stared at him. Now I was not only surprised but perplexed.

"Of course!" I said, notwithstanding, as I grabbed the broom he had pointed to and headed outside.

When I had managed to sweep a few leaves into a pile, a new gust of wind blew them all over.

After fifteen minutes I hadn't been able to clean up anything.

My old pastor was watching me amused, as if he were enjoying my plight and my increasing nervousness. Finally, he motioned with his hand for me to come over to him.

"Let's return to my office," he told me. "This wind is getting cold."

He went ahead of me, and soon we were sitting face-to-face again.

"You weren't able to do much, were you?"

"It's useless to try to sweep up these leaves until the wind stops."

"Exactly! That is what I wanted you to learn. Until the wind stops, it's better not to make any decisions about reorganizing our lives."

"What are you referring to?"

"Augustine of Hippo said it in these words: 'Do not make changes during times of storm.'"

And then he went on to explain it to me.

"Today you have been telling me about decisions you made during the night. Decisions that will affect your future and that of your wife. Listen to me."

He gaze was intense and penetrating.

"The dark nights of the soul, the times of storms, the winds that shake us up . . . . these are times when we must abide and trust, not make decisions."

"But, it's just that—"

"Not one decision," he interrupted me with unusual firmness, and he repeated it with absolute conviction. "Not one decision made in the middle of the night will be a right one. The very darkness of the vigil leaves us without any reference point from which to choose the right path. Stop, rest, trust, and wait until dawn comes."

"They have done us great harm," I insisted in my complaint. "They have been horribly unjust with us. All we have ever done is love and serve them, and look at how they have paid us—"

"Would you want to keep everybody at a distance from you?"

"That would be a great relief," I admitted out of woundedness.

"If you could, would you build a huge wall between them and your home?"

"I think I would, because—"

"Before you set up a barricade in your life," he interrupted me, insisting. "Before you build a wall, make sure you know what you are keeping inside, and remember that you will leave things on the outside as well."

He smiled at my perplexed expression, and then he said, "Listen to this story:

One day, a young man stopped in the center of a town and shouted that his heart was the most beautiful and perfect one in the whole region. A great crowd gathered around him, and they all admired and agreed that his heart was perfect. It did not have a single stain or one scratch. Yes, they all agreed that he had the most beautiful heart they had ever seen. Encouraged by all that praise, the young man shouted louder and louder that his heart was beautiful.

Then a small girl walked up and said, "I have seen a heart more beautiful than yours. It's the one that belongs to that old man." Surprised, they walked up to the old man and looked at his heart. Even though it was beating vigorously, it was full of scars, and even had places where some pieces were missing, which had been replaced by other parts that didn't fit perfectly in those places. They looked rough with irregular edges around them. In fact, there were still places with holes.

The young man gazed at the heart of the old man and then began to laugh. "You must be joking," he said to the little girl. "Compare that heart with mine. Mine is perfect, but that one is nothing but a mash of scars and hurts.

"Old man," he said to the man with contempt. "How is it that you have a heart that is in shambles?"

"It's true," said the old man. "My heart is in shambles. Every scar represents a person I gave my love to. I tore out pieces of my heart to give them to every person I've loved. At the same time, many of them have given me pieces of their hearts, which I placed in the open spots in my own heart. Since the pieces were not the same size, they had rough edges. But that makes me happy, because they remind me of the love we have shared. There were times when I gave a piece of my heart to someone, but that person didn't give me a piece of theirs in exchange. That explains the empty holes. To give love away is risky; but in spite of the pain these wounds that remain open have caused me, they remind me that I must continue to love them, because perhaps someday they will return and fill that emptiness."

The young man, moved by what he had heard, looked at the old man and then at the little girl, who said, "Do you now understand why I told you that this heart is more beautiful than yours?"

The young man was quiet, as tears ran down his cheeks. He drew near to the old man, tore out a piece of his beautiful and perfect heart, and offered it to him. The old man accepted it and placed it in his heart; then, in turn, he took a piece of his own, now old and ruined, and covered the open wound of the young man with it. The piece fit into the hole, but not perfectly. Since the pieces were not identical, you could see the edges. The young man looked at his heart, which was no longer perfect. But it seemed much more beautiful than before.

"I like that a lot more," said the little girl as she hugged the young man.[1]

My old pastor had finished his story. It was a conclusive message as usual.

"What do you think?" he asked. "Does it make sense? It's better to live loving others, don't you agree?"

Even the Dalai Lama hit the nail on the head when he said, "If you desire happiness from others, be compassionate. If you desire your own happiness, be compassionate."

"Yes, it is better to live loving others, even though in doing so you will have to pay a high price," assured my old pastor. "Look at the cross; it is the place that displays the most beautiful heart . . . but one that has been damaged beyond measure.

"Does it make sense?" my old pastor asked me.

He knew without any doubt that our discussions that afternoon had hit right on the mark, which is why he added, "Do you love those who despise you?"

He placed his hand on my chin, forcing me to raise my head so he could speak directly into my eyes. "Especially those who despise you. They are the ones who need it the most. Never harbor resentment, because resentment turns into bitterness that will end up killing you."

I lowered my head again, meditating on what I had just heard.

I wanted to run home and share it with Mary, but my old pastor had something else he wanted to say to me: "Those who serve others know that there are those who are really difficult to love.

It's true that the ideal of a servant is summed up as 'understand everything, love everyone, forgive everyone, and heal everyone.'"

He smiled, as if to calm me, and then added, "Nevertheless, this ideal hits reality with a head-on collision. There is no doubt that certain people provoke feelings of hostility, but there is an unquestionable truth: Behind a bad-tempered, demanding, tyrannical person is a suffering human being who has built up a thick shell of anger to fight against that pain. That shield can only be melted with the fire of love. A scowling, sour, disgruntled look often is a desperate cry that is saying, 'I need a smile!'"

"There are people so poor that the only thing they have is money," I said, remembering a saying that he himself had told me, "but there are others so rich that they have given themselves permission to go through life doling out smiles."

"Exactly," he agreed. "Feeling empathy toward a person who is shouting at us or threatening us is a difficult challenge for anyone, but if we succeed in putting ourselves in their place, grasping their suffering and understanding that their aggressive and disagreeable behavior is an awkward way of expressing their fear and emptiness, then we will be able to step in and help them effectively."

He patted my knee and then finished: "Love those who least deserve it more, because they are the ones who need it the most."

My old pastor's words brought to mind the risky statement by Sam Keen: "We come to love not by finding a perfect person, but by learning to see an imperfect person perfectly."

Perhaps this American philosopher was not so mistaken.

"Nevertheless," I objected as resolutely as I could, "constantly trying to empathize with divisive people wears out anybody's strength. At times I feel really worn out trying to understand, help, and smile at everyone."

"You're right," he admitted. "That's why we need to know how to skillfully manage the time we give to people. This is what I call the challenge of taking care of and renewing our spiritual resources. I had the good fortune a long time ago of having a book by Gordon MacDonald titled *Ordering Your Private World* fall into my hands. The author expresses some concepts that have helped me immensely in my attempt to maintain balance in the face of spiritual demands."

He pulled out a white sheet of paper from one of the pages of his Bible and prepared to write on it. Before he did, he explained, "According to MacDonald, during our time spent in ministry, we are going to come in contact with five kinds of people. These groups can be defined in categories by the effect they have in our lives. The ability to ration your time and the energy you spend with each one of them will greatly determine not only your effectiveness but also the length of your ministry."

He unfurled the sheet of paper and then picked up a fountain pen that caught my attention.

"That's interesting," I said, pointing to the pen. "It seems to be very old."

"As old as my ministry. It was a gift from my wife the day we were ordained to the pastorate. I have written almost all of my sermons with this simple instrument of metal and ink. It may be a funny old way, but I have never succeeded in getting used to those terrible contraptions of wires and keys."

"There are very small personal computers now," I pointed out. "They are completely portable and can be very useful."

"Computers." He wrinkled his brow. "I tried to use one of those gadgets one time, and the only thing it did was totally confuse me. Call me old-fashioned, but I wouldn't change my fountain pen for any of those inventions."

He wanted to focus my attention again on what was important, and so on the sheet spread out in front of him he drew a diagram with five parts. Then he turned the sheet toward me.

"Do you see these five groups?" he said to me. "They represent the five kinds of people whom I'm sure you already know and have made a part of your life:

"*People with problems*: They are everywhere, and you can be sure they're also in churches. They're not bad people. They're simply human beings who need help, and they will turn to you to find it. It may be a marriage that is in crisis, or a family whose head of the home has lost his job. It may be that person who suffers from various diseases and needs companionship and understanding, or that person who has lost a loved one. Once they have been restored, they can become precious disciples and even fellow warriors in battle. But that future hope does not eliminate the fact that this category is the one that produces the most wear and tear in our lives.

"*Good people*: They tend to make up the majority of the people in our congregations. They are the ones who faithfully come to every meeting. They don't come with any negative vibes or tend to cause problems. In fact, they contribute with their economic resources, and they support the projects in the church. Good people take up very little of our spiritual reserves. They like being around us because they enjoy what we have to offer them. The mere act of being around their pastors makes them feel good, but they, too, can slowly wear down our spiritual life.

"*Fellow battle warriors*: By this group I am referring to other servants who are involved in the same work. Perhaps pastors from other congregations or people who are involved in other ministries. They are friends who encourage and renew our faith. It is wise, positive, and necessary to cultivate relationships with them. We can relax around them because we know they are fellow battle warriors. In fact, we can laugh while we share stories about the ministry. We can also cry, and they will listen to us with compassion because the reality they are living is the same as ours. It's possible to exchange advice and experiences. Look for other leaders you can laugh, cry, and pray with. It will be healing and restoring.

"*Disciples*: You should dedicate a substantial part of your time to making disciples; that is, developing servants who grow under your influence, are skilled, and to whom you can delegate certain responsibilities. They are the men and women we have included in our most intimate inner circle so that they become our apprentices. If you're not making disciples, your church will not survive you. It will only last as long as you are there.

"*People with resources*: This is essential. This will be the kind of person who is capable of encouraging and reviving in us a passion for the ministry. When we are young, this is a role our pastor or wise people from the congregation can fulfill, but as we grow in our faith and ministerial experience, those who fulfill this kind of role in our lives will diminish. Perhaps our encouragement will come from our favorite author or perhaps from an intimate relationship with a mentor. Seek out people wiser than yourself. Allow them to nurture and feed you. It will be unlikely that you'll have many from this category, but seek them out. One hour spent with them can often provide encouragement that lasts weeks, months, or even years. Two hours with them will add several inches to your spiritual stature. I have not had more than four or five throughout my life, but they were influential in my ministry. They are mentors, people of experience who have already walked through the valley that you seem submerged in lately. They will teach you how to cope with hard times. Every minister should be able to identify at least two or three people who fulfill this place in his or her personal life."

He made sure I was paying attention while he pointed with the old fountain pen to each one of the groups and insisted, "These are the five kinds of people who will consume your time. It is very common that the people with problems and good people will fill our agendas 95 percent of the time. Because of that, it's not strange to feel that our resources are drained and that our ministry has very few long-term results. Without sources that restore our batteries, we can hardly maintain any forward movement in the different programs in our congregation or truly influence the lives of those who have been placed under our responsibility. This operative imbalance will produce tremendous ministerial, mental, and emotional wear and tear in us.

"The solution to this imbalance is fairly simple: we should apportion our time with wisdom and spend more time with the other three kinds of people: *people with resources, fellow battle warriors,* and *disciples.* This does not mean ignoring those who need us, but if we receive from and nurture ourselves with other relationships that contribute to our lives, we will be in a better condition to serve others."

At this point in his talk, he emphasized a number of times the expression *people with resources.*

"The proper management of our time," he went on, "along with wisdom in our relationships, will cause dry ministries to begin to grow again and revive the flames that have almost gone out."

The words of my old pastor made me remember the quote that James Hunter included in his magnificent book titled *The Paradox.* It's a story about the true essence of leadership, where he reflects, "It has taken almost my whole existence to learn that almost everything in this life has to do with relationships, relationships with God, yourself, and with others."

That was basically the same thing my old pastor told me that afternoon. The time had flown by, and I noticed he was tired, but I had been given so much and would have a lot to meditate on.

I got up from my chair, and he did the same.

Before I started to walk home, he put his hands on my shoulders, so that we were standing face-to-face, and he said to me, "Don't give up in the middle of the winter. Soldiers don't just die in wars, as it is glibly said. That is not how it happens. Each soldier dies in a very specific instant in a very specific battle. Mary and you are in a battle right now; don't let yourselves get killed in this skirmish."

His eyes were glowing with compassion, as well as his words.

"Never give up, because those who give up in the middle of winter will never enjoy another spring."

"At times winter can be so cruel that you can feel your soul shiver," I said, and I wasn't lying. "I'm not sure that Mary and I can bear it."

He squeezed my shoulders slightly—a gesture of closeness and a demonstration of attention at the same time.

"Do you respect your life?" he asked me, but he didn't let me answer. "I know that you do, son. Yours as well as your wife's. And also your church's. And since I know that you respect it, tell me this: have you gotten this far in your life, the only one you have and the only one you will ever have, to simply abandon it halfway through the race?"

His gaze remained fixed on my eyes.

"Are you really thinking of abandoning the seed you planted with excitement and hope? Will you leave the plow to which you fastened your life to be stuck in the middle of an abandoned field? Plant your feet solidly on the ground . . . your ground. Grab on to the plow firmly . . . your plow. Look straight ahead and continue planting because spring is drawing near."

In spite of everything, I smiled at my old pastor. Then I squeezed his hand on my shoulder and nodded.

He and Rachel said good-bye to me at the door. When they had shut the door, I noticed a fourth flower that was beginning to open on the rosebush.

Next to it three others with deep red petals swayed together, surrounded by white ones.

The night was warm and dark.

I felt full of victory. I was overflowing and wanted to run home and talk with Mary. Yet something compelled me to kneel down and worship, so I did, because I felt that a new flower was springing to life inside me, one that I liked, one that had always been thirsty and was quenching its thirst with the wise counsel from my old pastor and from quiet and sacred moments like the one I was enjoying right now.

I returned home completely renewed. Mary's smile told me that she was also feeling better.

"I'm sorry for upsetting you," she apologized as she hugged me. "I should be stronger."

I kissed her on the lips, stopping her from going on. Then I said to her, "You are strong, my love, very strong . . . and you demonstrate it every day."

She walked to the kitchen much calmer.

"It's time eat," she said as she set the plates on the small table that we had in the corner of the kitchen. "I have to get up early tomorrow. They need me early at the office—"

"Sweetheart," I interrupted her. "Do you know where that red notebook is?"

"You mean the one I bought last week to use as a recipe book in the kitchen?"

"Yes, that one. Have you started to write anything in it yet?"

"Not yet," she responded, surprised. "I thought of starting tomorrow with your favorite recipe: apple pie."

I picked up a pen with red ink.

Red notebook and red ink, I thought. *Nothing more appropriate to cover offenses with.*

"Bring it here, please," I asked her. "I suggest we use it for something different."

That night we surprised ourselves as together we wrote down names and details about offenses. The red ink seemed to glow on the white surface. And something began to glow inside us as well: a sparkle of forgiveness and an exuberant joy that began to drive out the shadows of resentment. But there's more. That night when I went to bed, I felt happiness. Its fragrance filled my nose. Its weight rested on my shoulders. I realized then how close forgiveness and happiness are to us.

I closed my eyes and slept, overtaken by a deep peace.

The Fifth Monday

Rips in the Soul

*What we may consider unpleasant storms often are gusts of
wind that redirect our ships to important ports that we never
would have reached if we had had a pleasant crossing.*

H ow is Mary?" my old pastor asked me when he saw me
that next Monday.

He was referring to the discouragement that had taken up
our time during our last meeting.

"She's fine. Thank God she has recovered from that 'existen-
tial crisis,'" I joked.

"Love her a lot," he told me, "and don't forget to tell her that
often."

I noticed that he was staring intensely at a small picture on
the table. It was inside a simple wooden frame.

From the very first day I had visited him in his office, it had caught my attention, though I had never dared ask him about the smiling little boy in the picture.

I kept looking at that face, blond and cheerful, and his features reminded me of those of my old pastor. The expression of the small boy was sweet, and his smile had two rows of very white, tiny, and perfectly aligned teeth. He was sitting on my old pastor's knees, and Rachel, off to one side, was watching them with the pride of one who was contemplating a valuable trophy.

"Joseph."

"Excuse me?" His voice made me jump.

"The little boy," he pointed out. "His name was Joseph."

"Was . . . ?" I asked.

"He died when he was eleven," he answered me almost in a whisper.

Unable to hide my expression of surprise, I looked at his face as he stood in front of the large window. For a moment, it seemed to me that he was sniffling as tears began to shine briefly in his eyes.

"It is natural to die," he spoke in a low tone, and I had to lean closer to hear him. "But there is a logical order. First, it should be parents and then children." He turned his gaze from the horizon to focus his eyes on me with a shocking fixation.

"But there are times when that order gets altered. For reasons that escape us, it gets turned upside down and turns into a blow with terrible pain. You have no idea of the feeling of absurdity and emptiness that happens when you have to bury a son, especially if you already shared some of your years of life with him. I mean those who have already grown up. Those with whom we have spent times of laughter and crying. Those we have played soccer with or romped together with on the living room floor; those who have left indelible imprints on our memories."

He breathed in deeply, and after taking that breath, he coughed, but it wasn't a cough—rather a sob that rose in his throat. Then he became silent. I knew then that the pain of absence is not always healed with time, that past scratches leave inevitable grooves on the delicate fabric of the memory.

I could not stop the words of Baltasar Gracián from ringing in my mind: "For young people, death is a shipwreck, but for old people it is reaching port." I could tell that this shipwreck had left those who remained behind aimlessly adrift rather than those who had gone on.

The old man remained silent, and I felt as though I had to say something—to offer him some word of comfort—but nothing came out. He must have noticed my inability to say something coherent, because mercifully, he went on: "He died."

His fingers were visibly trembling as he stroked the picture of that little boy who looked like my old pastor.

"God decided to transplant the most beautiful flower from our garden to His."

I was going to ask him a question, but the old man started up again, without giving me the chance.

"It was not easy to get used to the blow." He looked at me, focusing his eyes on mine. "I even got angry with God!"

He lowered his head, then in a lower voice he added, "How stupid of me to think I was worthy to ask God to explain Himself. It was in that moment that an old story came to me. Would you like me to tell it to you?"

He did not wait for me to answer. Instead, he began his story:

It is said that one day there was a peasant who asked God if he could rule over nature, so that it would produce better crops for Him. And God granted him his wish! From that moment on, when the peasant wanted a light rain, it happened; when he asked for sunshine, the celestial king of the sky shone in all its splendor; if he needed water, it rained harder.

But when the time of harvest came, his surprise and shock were great, because it was a complete failure. Upset and angry, he asked God why the experiment had ended that way. Why did the crop turn out bad, since he had asked for what he thought was the perfect weather?

God answered him, "You asked for what you wanted, but in reality that wasn't what was needed. You never asked for a storm, and those are necessary to cleanse the sowing of the seed, to scare away the birds and animals that destroy it, and to purify it from the pestilences that are very destructive."

Once again he fixed his gaze on me, and a holy and contagious passion lit up from the depth of his eyes.

"That's how it happens to us often," he said. "We want our lives to be pure nectar without any problems. An abundance of honey and a complete absence of bitterness. A true winner is not someone who does not see difficulties but rather one who is not frightened by them and does not retreat or turn back. That's why we can declare without fear of being wrong that difficulties are advantageous. They produce maturity and growth. Every person needs a real storm in his life to make him understand how much he has worried about light showers and simple fleeting nonsense. The important thing is not to flee from the storm but rather to have faith and trust that it will pass and will leave something good in our lives."

"Pastor," I said, hesitating a moment, but then I knew that I had to ask him the question. With an almost irresponsible boldness, I asked, "What happened to Joseph? I mean, how did he die?"

The old man took a breath, looked at me, and knew my interest was sincere. Finally, the words hesitantly came through the floodgate of his lips: "I've never liked driving at night, but I had no choice but to return home. I drove very slowly, and my car never went more than fifty miles per hour. I've always thought that driving with good judgment and moderation is the safest way to arrive faster."

He turned his head for a moment. Then he looked straight ahead again.

"The driver that was coming in the other direction did not think the same way as I did. That's why he took the curve too fast and crossed over into our lane and hit us head-on."

He stopped for a moment and breathed in deeply, as if all his breath had been spent in the first part of the story.

"Rachel was sitting beside me and screamed. I screamed as well, but from the backseat where Joseph was, there was only silence. The next thing I remember was that Joseph was in my arms. He was quiet and not breathing. His silence and stillness were all that my senses detected. I started to shake him, though he had no spark of life in him. I called him back to life: 'Joseph!

Son!' I shouted. 'Wake up! You're here with me,' I kept shouting. 'You're with Daddy!' Two men took him from my arms and carried him off as if they still could do something for him. Before they took him away from me, I said to him softly, almost stupidly, 'Joseph, my life, we will see each other soon.' And I stayed on the ground, sitting on the asphalt. But since then I have thought about it, and perhaps what I said to him was not that stupid . . . that 'we will see each other soon.'"

The silence went on as if he wasn't going to say anything else. But I knew that he would go on, so instead of answering him this time, I remained quiet and kept my hand on his shoulder.

"A nurse came to take care of me. She took my right hand and asked me if it hurt. I asked her about Rachel. Only after they assured me that she was fine and that they had given her some sedatives because she was very nervous but all right . . . only then did I look at my hand. It was bleeding and had a gash that started on the back and went halfway up my forearm."

He showed me the scar that was still very noticeable, despite the years that had gone by since then.

"The nurse bandaged it, but she was more worried about it than I was. I was feeling another wound instead. It was a crushing pain in my chest. I opened my jacket. A shard of twisted metal had smashed into my chest against my pocket Bible. That book, which had saved my life, was now a jumble of torn pages that fell to the ground, and the wind whipped them around in every direction. But the other wound . . . the one deep inside . . . the one caused by Joseph's silence . . . God, how that hurt!"

"It must have been very hard," was all that I could say.

He took so long to respond that I thought he never would.

He finally continued his story with his eyes fixed on the horizon, on that spot where the sky and earth blend together, as if he were projecting the facts out there. "Those are not just scratches but rather rips in the soul. After Joseph's funeral, Rachel and I would go to bed early, sometimes when it was only dusk, when the day was hardly starting to close its eyelids. We would go to bed early because we wanted to shorten the days as much as we could. But shortening the days only made the darkness of the nights longer. The nights took weeks to end. Some were almost unending; each minute turned into a century."

He got quiet for a moment and turned his head toward me. Then he went on. "We tried to turn off the lamp of memory . . . trying not to remember anything, but it was impossible to dim the light of those moments lived with our little Joseph. We felt every second of his absence like bites that filled our skin with sores. In one sense, you never recover. You are never the same. Your mind is full of questions, and your heart also looks desperately for answers . . . in vain. How right Dostoevsky was! 'It is only when we have said good-bye that we feel and understand the strength with which we have loved.'"

It was getting dark, casting shadows on the countryside. The falling darkness outside made the inside reflect in the windowpanes. I saw his face in those reflections and noticed that the shining in his eyes had become a stream of tears running down his cheeks. I understood the essence of that phrase that someone had quoted to me one time: "Often, the grave buries two hearts in the coffin without knowing it."

It was terrible to see a good man, and one full of wisdom, at the mercy of such tragedy. The old man was sunk down in his reading chair, his head bent down, pensive, discouraged as never before.

Yet to my surprise, he quickly composed himself. Sitting up a little in his chair and gathering up admirable energy, he said, "But what is indisputable, what no one should ever doubt, is when the winter intensifies, God draws near to us and wraps us and keeps us warm. The miracle of His presence fills the hole of any emptiness, even the most atrocious ones . . . even those losses that leave you adrift, asking yourself if someday you will ever be able to piece yourself back together."

The one who was speaking now was not the old defeated man from a moment ago. From behind the moisture of his eyes, a warm and calm brightness peered out, like the sun after a night of storms.

"The hand of God turns the ruins of the soul into works of art. When He shows up, He firmly grabs hold of the rudder of our lives and guides our ships toward a safe harbor."

Impressed by his words, I said in a triumphant tone, "And He did it with you, isn't that right?"

"As a matter of fact, He did," he declared. "You're absolutely correct. It's not about forgetting your loved one who is gone . . . absolutely not! The memory is always there, and I'm not going to hide the fact from you that an old wound that you think has healed over can't open up and bleed again. But I have come to understand that when God erases something, it's because He is going to write something new."

His words filled his face with hope. Mine too. And they restored his usual strength.

"I managed to understand that death is just a change in mission and that our little Joseph is more alive than ever, because if death weren't a prelude to another life, then this present life would be a cruel joke."

He did not say it as a matter of fact; he declared it with triumph.

Outside, the sky was dotted with clouds, and surprisingly, the sun, which could be seen behind them as a red half circle touching the horizon, filtered its sharp beams of light through the cottony cumulus clouds, forming a perfect fan.

"There you see it," he said, pointing out that scenery. "He's drawing beautiful pictures on dark canvases. What a perfect artist God is! His brush changes that which threatens into perfect beauty. God will never waste one sorrow. Instead, He will turn it into riches."

That phrase, spoken with transparent sincerity in the face of such a difficult circumstance, was decisive for the future of my faith. It has echoed so many times in the depths of my conscience, and it has always helped to lift me up in the face of adversity that threatened to knock me down.

He looked at me, and his lips curved into a smile that shone with more light than a thousand dawns. Nodding his head slightly, he said, "You know? One time I spoke with a friend who achieved the feat of scaling a mountain twenty-three thousand feet high. 'What did you feel?' I asked him. 'Cold,' he answered, 'mostly cold. During the day the sky is more dark than blue because it lacks the air to reflect the sun's light. But at night, you have never seen so many stars. It's as if you could touch them, and they shine so brightly that they seem like holes in heaven's floor. The other thing is the silence. When you're up there at the highest place in the world, you will experience true silence . . . and then I heard the sound of the mountain, as if I had heard the voice of God.'"

The words of my old pastor touched me and were warm and overwhelming. They seemed like the breath of a bonfire more than words. He was speaking with a true anointing.

"Height carries with itself certain risks, and the situations of life that make us grow and scale high places often place us under dark skies. A dark mountain pass, which lifts us up, also places us where we will experience cold and loneliness, but that's where we discover that there are hidden treasures in the folds of its shadows."

He kept silent for a moment to allow me to process the information he was giving to me. Then he continued, "Only there will we appreciate that the night is full of light, and the silence is saturated with voices that speak forth wisdom."

His talk had an undeniable beauty about it, but I could not take my eyes off those of the young boy who smiled at me from the photograph. Deep inside I tried to gauge the pain they must have faced in losing him.

"Pastor, I empathize with what you're telling me, but you can't deny that at times God does things . . ." I faltered, "or allows certain moves on the chessboards of our lives that are difficult to understand and extremely complicated to grasp."

"Would you want to know everything that's going to happen?" he asked kindly.

"That's not it, but—"

"You've just given me the opportunity to tell you a story." He wiped away with determination the warm tears that spilled from his eyes, and smiled. "Would you like to hear it?"

I nodded, and he stirred a bit in his chair and began his story:

The teacher always told a parable at the end of every class, but the students didn't always understand the meaning. "Teacher," one of the students challenged him, "you tell us stories, but you don't explain their meaning."

"I'm sorry," the teacher apologized. "As a way of making it up to you, let me invite you to have a ripe peach to eat."

"Thank you, Teacher," the student answered, flattered.

"To make this a special feast for you, I would like to peel your peach for you myself. May I?"

"Yes, thank you," said the student.

"Since I already have the knife in my hand, would you like me to cut it into pieces so it's easier for you to eat?"

"I would love that, but I wouldn't want to take advantage of your generosity."

"It's not taking advantage if I'm the one offering it. I only want to please you. Allow me to chew it before I give it to you."

"No, Teacher. I don't want you to do that!" the disciple objected, surprised.

The Teacher paused. "If I explain the meaning of each story to all of you, it would be like giving you a fruit already chewed."

The story was finished, and my old pastor focused his gaze on me. "If God allowed us to understand everything that happens to us," he said, "it would be like eating fruit that has already been chewed."

I nodded my head as I meditated on the profound wisdom that could be gleaned from such a simple story.

"Don't despair if you don't understand the meaning of something today. Keep eating the fruit. This is also the message of the cross."

He pointed to the dozen crucifixes that decorated that simple room. "We do not understand what happened there until we visit the tomb and find it empty. Too often we despair and give up in the middle of the storm, when the only thing we should do is trust and wait. The storm will pass, and then we will discover that the waves that terrified us were actually the same waves that served to alter the course of our sailing, causing us to dock in the right harbor."

"Do you mean to say that He uses storms to steer us in the right direction?"

"And tears to clear our vision. As Lord Byron said, 'One can see further through a tear than through a telescope.' Wisdom is understanding that the rain that soaks our bodies and stains winter gray is heaven's paint—green, pink, yellow—and the tumultuous winds that shake us stir up the oil, which gives it the necessary consistency to be used by spring's paintbrush. It is only a question of waiting, and our surroundings will fill up with color."

I nodded in admiration at his wisdom.

"On the other hand," he added, "you will come to understand

that your scars will form part of your credentials for the ministry. It's easy to serve when everything is going well, but the hard times in life will lend credibility to your service and depth to your words."

He smiled as he concluded, "Don't trust too much in the speech of a man who doesn't have scars. That's one of the greatest risks that the church faces."

He rubbed his chin in thought, thinking about his next words.

"One of the things that can kill a congregation is to be led by people who have miles of influence but only inches of depth. Trials and adversities make us mature. Times of drought cause us to sink our roots deep down into the earth looking for water. That lends credibility to your ministry."

I looked at him intently, and a certainty overwhelmed me that many of the wrinkles that furrowed his face were not just folds of skin but also battle scars.

Once again he had turned his face toward the large window. I watched his reflection in the glass as he reflected on a saying by Arthur Miller: "I don't ever regret having risked everything for what was important to me."

This was the caliber of man my old pastor was. And that is why his discourse carried so much weight . . . and the reason his words were full of such wisdom.

"Don't endure the cross. Love it. Do you still have any strength to endure another story?"

The look in his eyes was almost apologetic, and his facial expression seemed gracefully childlike. "I warned you that I have a lot to say and few ears willing to listen."

"Well, you have an eager listener," I assured him.
And so he began:

A certain man was burdened down with a heavy cross. He was dragging it along with anger and resignation. Many people had informed him that the cross was lighter for the one who carries it than for the one who drags it, but he would not listen to their advice and continued to drag his cross along bitterly. It would get caught in the rocks on the road and tangled with the weeds, making his progress difficult.

One day he crossed a desert place, so wide and dry he thought he would die. The merciless sun burned his head and scorched his back. It was by chance that he positioned himself so that the cross came between his body and the sun, and he discovered that his heavy burden provided him shade. Surprised by the pleasant discovery, he nestled up, protecting himself behind the wood.

Days later he began to feel very hungry. During his crossing through the desert, he had hardly eaten anything, and he looked weak and malnourished. He noticed a lush apple tree filled with fruit, but the juicy apples were too high up for him to reach. The sight of that fruit increased his appetite, and the poor man regretted having so much fruit in front of him and not being able to enjoy it. Complaining and rather desperate, he leaned the cross up against the trunk of the tree and sat on the ground feeling bad. When he looked up, he discovered that that wooden cross could be used as a ladder for him to reach the fruit. That's what he did, and he ate until he was full.

A little while later, on his long trip, he crossed an inhospitable stretch of snow-covered land. The cross got stuck in the snow, and progress became very slow and very hard. Suddenly, he heard the howling of wolves and felt a shudder of fear. They were very close, and he knew they were looking for him. Soon he could hear the rapid approach of those hungry wild beasts. He started to run, but dragging the cross behind him made his running difficult. A number of times he thought of leaving it behind, but the firm pledge he had made to carry it the rest of his life made him dismiss that idea.

He decided to pick it up and run with it. He discovered that it was lighter that way. He ran and ran, yet sensing that the wild beats were getting closer. Suddenly, he stopped dead. Right in front of him lay an abyss—a deep, dried-up riverbed. He desperately looked for a bridge but couldn't find one. The wolves were getting closer, and he burst into tears. Trapped by fury and anger he threw the cross to the side. And before his eyes, which were as wide as saucers, as the cross fell, it stretched from one edge to the other of that dry riverbed . . . forming a bridge. He quickly crossed over, and as he picked up the cross again, he watched as the wolves, on the other side, slunk away disappointed. From that day on, he lived embracing the cross, and he made it the center of his life.

"Love the cross that God brings into your life," my old pastor told me, "whatever it is. At times the cross takes the shape of a sickness. At other times it takes on the incredible weight of loneliness or economic hardship. Carrying your cross implies paying a price, but I assure you, it's worth it. It won't be long before you discover that cross turning into a ladder that will lift you up to new heights or place you in the shade that will protect you in the midst of extreme circumstances."

Still holding the picture of Joseph to his chest, he changed the subject. It was such a radical change that it caught me by surprise, leaving me a bit perplexed.

"Love her," he said to me. "Love Mary. Never hold back from offering your love to those closest to you, because you never know when those who are near today will no longer be around. Love her today. Express it today. Hug her today. Don't say that's too soon to do it, because you don't know if it soon might be too late. Get up early to express your love, because at times night comes too quickly, cutting in half the most beautiful day, and then the words you should have said are trapped. They leap from the throat to the conscience, and there they remain, like an intolerable weight."

And as he said it, he squeezed the photo of his absent son tightly to his heart.

At that moment, Rachel entered with a tray on which she carried steaming coffee. On seeing him holding that picture, she left the tray on the table, sat down beside her husband, and hugged him tenderly for a long time.

Seeing them this way, I realized that no matter how great the loss is, God never allows us to utterly despair. He always leaves sufficient doses of love at our side.

I wiped away a tear with the back of my hand before looking at them again.

They were still holding each other in a long embrace, and as I watched them, I was even surer of the fact that God does not leave us as orphans or drifting aimlessly. I thought also that at times we miss out on life longing for the embrace of someone who has died without realizing that there are a thousand hugs around us that want to clothe us in our coldest night of the soul.

The words of the wise Indian poet echoed in my mind: "If you cry at night because you can't see the sun, your tears will prevent you from seeing the stars."[1]

I wanted to run home and find Mary. With all my strength, I wanted to show her my appreciation and hug her that day.

I wanted all my declarations of love to be said in time. I didn't want any word of appreciation or a single expression of love to be trapped in my throat only to later weigh heavily on my conscience.

The visit had been short but intense. I was not surprised to discover a new red rose opening up that quiet summer night.

I took one of its petals between my fingers and appreciated its beauty and perfection as I whispered, "There is always something that shines in the night, and even the most terrible darkness can be the womb from which a new day is birthed. There are stars sheltered inside the folds of shadows."

The Sixth Monday

My Wife Is Deaf

Watch and guard the health of your family. One of the most powerful credentials of a ministry is your marriage.

This time I couldn't wait until Monday, so I decided to call my old pastor on the phone. What was the reason for such urgency? I was mad . . . really mad with my wife, Mary. It doesn't happen often, but the night before it did. It was like two trains hitting head-on, and the worst of it is that it was over something trivial—as foolish as to whether we should buy a new chair for the living room.

Unable to deal with the problem by myself, I dared to bother my pastor.

"I think Mary is a little disturbed," I blurted out to him as soon as he picked up the phone.

"She's what?"

"Crazy in the head—a little out of balance."

"Why do you say that?"

"I suggested to her that we change the chair, and she got all tangled up in arguing like a lunatic. There was no way I could get her to listen to reason."

"Did you ask her why she was acting that way?"

"Of course I asked her, but I don't remember now what foolish thing she answered."

"And she rejected all your arguments."

"Yes. She said, for example, that my idea of wanting to change the chair was stupid."

"Really. Or that you're always changing your mind."

"That too! How did you know?"

"Wait, wait!" he said to me. "Let me tell you a joke!"

I was perplexed by my pastor's reaction, but out of respect, I got ready to listen to him.

A man called the family doctor. "Doctor, come at once. I'm worried about my wife."

"What's wrong with her?"

"She's going deaf."

"What do you mean she's going deaf?"

"She really is. I need you to come see her."

"Look," the doctor argued. "Generally, deafness is not something that comes on so fast or severe, so bring her to the office on Monday, and I will see her."

"But do you think we can wait until next Monday?"

"What makes you think she can't hear?"

"Well . . . because when I call her she doesn't answer."

"Look, it can be a simple thing, like an earplug in the ear. First of all, let's do something. We're going to determine the level of deafness your wife has. Where are you?"

"In the bedroom."

"And where is she?"

"In the living room."

"Great, so call her from there."

"Carmeeen! No, she doesn't hear me."

"Okay, go closer to the bedroom door and shout from the hallway."

"Carmeeen! No, not even now."

"Don't be too concerned. Go get the cordless phone and go into the hallway and call her to see if she hears you."

"Carmeeen! Carmeeen! Carmeeen! Nothing's happening. I'm in front of the door of the living room and I see her. She has her back turned to me and is reading a book, but she doesn't hear me. Carmeeen! Nothing's happening."

"Go closer."

The man entered the room, walked up to Carmen, put his hand on her shoulder, and shouted in her ear: "Carmeeen!"

The wife, furious, turned around and said to him: "What do you want? What do you want? What do you wannnnt? You've called me about ten times, and ten times I've answered you, 'What do you want?' You're getting deafer by the day. I don't know why you don't go to the doctor."

"That is what I call projection, my son. Every time I see something that bothers me in another person, I remember that what I see, at the very least, is something I can have the same issue with as well. But forgive me for interrupting you, let's get back to . . . what were you telling me about Mary's head?"

I was speechless.

This was an aspect about my old pastor that I wasn't aware of: his irony.

Feeling that my cheeks were burning, I decided to redouble my use of tolerance with others and use a little more self-criticism.

"Nothing, Pastor," I said to him, feeling quite chagrined. "I'll see you next Monday, God willing . . ."

On the next visit, I confessed to my pastor my feelings about the episode with Mary. He laughed hard as he patted me on the back. Though I must say I noticed he was tired.

I was very worried about my old pastor's health. As I watched him for a moment, it seemed to me as if he was a person whose life was about over, like an athlete who has given his all in a race and finds himself exhausted on the last curve of the track. Nevertheless, when he began to talk, and especially when he prayed, you could appreciate the superhuman strength he possessed . . . something that transcended that which was merely of this earth.

I have absolutely no doubt: he lived very close to God, and that is what gave him unquestionable authority.

"We all make mistakes," he said when he had finished laughing. "The only necessary thing is to know how to recognize it. And never forget what I told you on our last visit: love her, and do it in such a manner that infidelity is not an option and that the possibility of betraying her never enters your mind. Leo Tolstoy said many things that I don't agree with, but on occasion he hit it on the head, like when he declared: 'He who has known his wife and has loved her, knows more about women than he who has known a thousand.'"

"You and Rachel have been together many years—"

"Sixty," he interrupted me. "And they have gone by in a flash."

"Yet it seems that you two have loved each other just as much since the first day. What is your secret?"

"I just remembered a story . . ."

His face took on an expression as if he were asking for forgiveness.

"Please understand, I'm not trying to dodge your question, but lately my memory has become a bit fuzzy, and I may not be able to remember it later."

He took my smile as consent, so he began his story:

A man went to visit a wise counselor and told him he no longer loved his wife and was thinking of getting a separation. The wise man listened to him, looked him in the eyes, and only said two words to him: "Love her." Then he kept quiet.

"But I don't have feelings for her anymore."

"Love her," the wise man said again. And standing there in front of the distressed man, after another prolonged silence, he added the following: "Love is a decision, not a feeling; love is dedication and surrender. To love is a verb, and the fruit of that action is love. Love is an exercise in gardening: you tear out what causes damage, you prepare the ground, you sow, then you are patient as you water and take care of it. Be prepared because there will be plagues, droughts, or excessive rain, but you don't give up on your

garden because of them. Love your wife: that is, accept her, value her, respect her, give her your affection, admire her and understand her. That is everything—love her."

After a few seconds of silence, he said to me, "Robert Anderson gave a very interesting key for a stable marriage. He said this: 'In every marriage more than a week old, there are grounds for divorce. The trick is to find, and continue to find, grounds for marriage.'"

He smiled at me, and when I had smiled back, he went on. "The only pillar capable of supporting the weight of a marriage is love. Only love is the pillar that is able to hold up that building during cruel winters and against the most adverse conditions. And perhaps you will ask yourself, 'What does this romantic theme have to do with the solemn issues of the ministry?'"

"Well," I ventured, "marriage is related to ministry . . ."

"Marriage *is* the ministry." He strongly emphasized the verb *is.* "One of the most powerful credentials of the ministry is your marriage. A healthy love life reinforces and strengthens the ministerial area. Taking care of your family is taking care of your church. And the key to that care is love: Lavish love on your loved ones. Love with abundance; give away your love with no limits."

"God is love," I said, remembering. "Does that have anything to do with it?"

"'Of course," he congratulated me. "The relationship that God has with us is based on what His own essence is: love. That is why He continues to seek us out in spite of our insolence, indifference, and contempt. He loves us and forgives us. That is the key for a marriage, to keep on loving 'in spite of.' To keep on forgiving."

"In spite of," I repeated. "That seems like an interesting point to me."

"Something falls short with the concept of love," he said with conviction as he opened his Bible and thumbed through the pages with admirable agility. "I have discovered that there are two types of love. Listen to what 1 Samuel 1:5 says: 'But to Hannah he would give a double portion, for he loved Hannah, although the LORD had closed her womb.'"

My old pastor explained, "The story is about a man named Elkanah who had a wife named Hannah. The Bible says that this woman could not have children—that is, she was barren."

He leaned over toward me to explain more thoroughly: "To capture the real meaning of this verse, you need to know that in that time and culture, the rabbis said there were ten types of people who were excluded from a relationship with God. They were people who had been labeled . . . considered cursed. That relationship began with that man who did not have a wife, or having one, she could not give him sons. There is no doubt that Hannah's barrenness represented a serious problem, not just for her but for her husband as well. The state of a man whose wife was barren turned him into something similar to being anathema . . . one who was cursed and excluded from communion with God."

"Really!" I replied, recognizing that was a real problem.

"Nevertheless," he affirmed, "the text that we have read contains an exciting phrase that is worth considering. 'But to Hannah he would give a double portion, for *he loved Hannah, although* the LORD had closed her womb.'"

I noticed that in his Bible the phrase "for he loved Hannah, although" was underlined several times, as if he had gone back to that Bible text at different times.

"As I told you, I have observed that there are two types of love," he continued. "There's *love because*. I love you *because* I find complete satisfaction in you. *Because* you fulfill all my expectations, *because* with you I am totally happy ... I love you *because* ... That is a legitimate love. It is always better to love *because* than not to love at all. But this kind of love always has another side to it. It does not give of itself wholeheartedly. This kind of love inevitably has an expiration date."

His look, which was fixed on me, was inquisitive, seeking to discern if I was grasping the intensity of what he was trying to convey to me.

"There is a higher option that is worthy and long-lasting: there's *love although*. It's a love 'in spite of.' I love you *although* you can't always fulfill my expectations, *although* you are not perfect. This is the kind of love described in 1 Corinthians 13. It is the kind of love that does not have an expiration date, and therefore, it is able to support the weight of a marriage. This is the kind of love that God declares to us in Romans 5:8: 'But God demonstrates His own love toward us, in that while we were still sinners, Christ died for us.'"

"That is really interesting," I admitted.

"There are people who say, 'We don't love each other anymore' or 'our love ended,' and they say it with all sincerity, suffering. In every case that I have observed, the kind of love that has worn out is the *love because*. No one is capable of always fulfilling their loved one's expectations. A time will come when we fail, when we are not at our best at loving fully. At some point we will offend them or let them down. The *love because* becomes resentful at these times, but the *love although* covers these valleys with bridges of forgiveness and fills the potholes with understanding . . . This is the love that God declares to us. As Leibniz affirmed, 'To love is to find your own happiness in the happiness of another.'"

"Will God ever get tired of forgiving us?" I asked, although I already anticipated his answer.

"Pray that that is not the case. His heart is attached to ours beyond measure. He is the Creator who is madly in love with His creatures. He is a Redeemer irremediably in love with His redeemed. Let me tell you a story:

An Arabic legend tells of two friends who were traveling through the desert, and when they had arrived at a certain point in their journey, they started to argue. One of them, offended and not wanting to speak, wrote in the sand: Today, my best friend slapped me on the face.

They went on and reached an oasis, where they decided to bathe. The one who had been slapped was about to drown, but he was saved by his friend. After recovering, he took his stiletto and carved on a rock: Today, my best friend saved my life.

Intrigued, his friend asked, "Why did you write in the sand after I hurt you, and now you are carving on a stone?"

Smiling, his friend answered: "Because you are my friend, and your offenses I write in the sand, where the winds of forgetfulness and forgiveness take care of erasing them. But I carve your help and love on the stone of memory of my heart, where no wind in all the world will be able to erase it."[1]

My old pastor waited a few seconds for me to take in the message contained in the story, and then he said, "There are two things to learn that are important keys for life: The first is that forgiveness is the foundation stone for a marriage. The second is that whatever offense, whatever failure we have committed against God, no matter how serious, cannot stand up against the water of repentance and the purification by the blood of Jesus."

He stood, and I knew that our meeting had come to an end.

"Well," he said, "I am going to stop bothering you with so much chatter. I must have made you dizzy by now."

I would have liked to reply to him that he wasn't bothering me. On the contrary, everything he was telling me I not only found interesting—because I was learning things I hadn't been able to learn with anyone else—but it was much more than that, because many of his words were like powerful lights . . . authentic lighthouses . . . in the middle of my confusion.

He accompanied me to the door, walking very slowly and with noticeable difficulty. From there I watched as he walked away, waving good-bye.

I had only taken about five steps when I heard his voice trying to get my attention. "You know, son?"

I stopped and looked at him. Then he said, "To have a good marriage, you have to fall in love many times"—he made a strategic pause before finishing—"always with the same person."

He was laughing as he closed the door. Then everything went silent.

I retraced my steps and took a deep breath as I bent down

next to the rosebush. The sixth red rose was opening up among its companions.

The silence of that place was like a comfortable cloak that isolated me from everything and invited me to reflect on what I had just heard.

These meetings with my old pastor were transforming me. There was so much wisdom to be gleaned from his experience! He had known a lot of people during his long years, but what I appreciated about my old pastor was that his long years were filled with life.

How fortunate he and Rachel were!

I stopped and smiled at my remark. Fortunate? That was not exactly right . . . on the contrary, they were wise. They had chosen well where to live. They had picked a place where each day of their lives was filled with meaning, and that place was the cross.

They had decided to lay the foundation of their home in the shade of the cross.

I returned home very slowly, almost meandering through the countryside. I was feeling so much peace! And all the advice was being filed away on the hard drive of my memory.

I really do love Mary . . . This last thought acted like spurs in my heart, making me pick up my pace.

A little while later, both the night and I arrived home at the same time.

The Seventh Monday

Admirable Faith

If you want a healthy and solid church, do not focus on what astounds but rather on what transforms. Preach the Bible.

Weeks went by before I saw him again—two weeks because of my responsibilities and two other weeks because of his precarious health.

"If there is anything I can help you with . . ." I offered when Rachel told me over the phone that her husband was sick and couldn't see me that week.

"I appreciate that," she told me. "The only thing he needs is rest."

Yet I somehow knew that my dear pastor's poor health had something more to it than being tired.

A few days later the telephone rang, and I was invited to come the following Monday.

When I arrived, the heat was crashing down on that place, and the sun, asserting its absolute rule at times, was buffeting each of the four sides of the house.

The whitewashed walls were glaring brightly beneath the sun's rays. I was surprised that in spite of the heat, the rosebush in the tub was fresh and lush. The red roses were still very fresh, and their petals seemed like glass.

How is it possible that they don't wilt? I thought.

The garden was a little untidy, and the grass was longer than usual, which I thought strange.

"Good afternoon. I'm happy to see you again," Rachel greeted me, appearing more tired than usual. As I had expected, my old pastor had not come to the door to welcome me.

"If you don't mind," she said to me, "you can talk to him in his room today. He's lying down, but he's waiting for you anxiously."

I lightly tapped her back so she would stop. "What's the matter with your husband, Rachel?" My worry had caused me to cross the line of discretion. "I know there's something seriously wrong with him. Please tell me what it is."

She lowered her head and held it there for almost a whole minute. The slight shaking of her shoulders made me realize that Rachel was crying. For a few seconds I regretted having asked her, and I didn't know what to do. Finally, timidly and hesitantly, I rested my hand on her shoulder and left it there, trying to convey that she wasn't alone.

Rachel straightened up and lifted her head. The brightness in her eyes today wasn't the result of determination.

"Cancer," she managed to say.

Only one word, but as sharp as a stiletto and as destructive as a bomb.

If I didn't know what to do at her tears, I found it impossible now to know what to say. I leaned up against the wall in the short hallway trying to compose my shaken feelings.

"Is it serous?" I bit my lips as I realized how absurd my question was.

A few moments of silence passed, but I was no longer waiting for her answer. Finally, she spoke, but her voice was just a whisper: "Two months; with any luck, four. The tumor was very hidden, and by the time it appeared, it had already left its mark on many vital organs."

My heart leaped into my throat as if I were choking up pain. My eyes were fixed on Rachel, but I couldn't see her. My state of shock kept me dumbstruck for a long time, until finally I was able to ask, "I assume that he will have the best doctors, right?"

"Of course, but still, it's not an easy sickness to endure."

"Does he know?"

"Since the very first moment, and he has endured it with a sweet serenity." The smile that returned to Rachel's face was also just as sweet, lighting it up. "His faith is a pillar that keeps his building intact and a flagpole that holds his flag high."

"That phrase sounds familiar," I said. "I think he used it in one of his sermons."

"He preached it several times, and now he is demonstrating that he knows how to live what he preaches. Three months ago he started to show some very noticeable symptoms, and from the beginning he knew it was something serious, but I have never seen him waver."

"Where does he find his strength?"

"In the cross." She didn't hesitate in answering with absolute assurance. "The cross is his harbor of rest. There he heals his wounds, rests, and is restored."

"Your husband loves God deeply," I said to Rachel.

"And he feels loved by Him."

She was speaking with devotion.

"When the pain squeezes in, he repeats sweetly: 'He suffered more for me . . . The cross was harder, and He did it for love.'" She ended the sentence again with a smile.

"It pleases me to see you smile."

"I love smiling," she said to me.

"It's good to smile," I agreed. "I've heard that it activates a group of muscles and hormones that produce an essential therapeutic effect. Yet I can't help admire people like you who are capable of doing it in the midst of pain."

"I do it for my own good, and also for the good of my husband," she said. "Smiling produces sanity, not only for the one who receives it but for the one who gives it as well. That is a fact. Just as it is that there are emotions that have a debilitating effect on the body, such as fear, distrust, hate, envy, guilt . . ."

She looked at me and smiled again.

"Flee from those feelings like the plague, but don't flee from smiling. Smile even when you don't want to. It is the easiest gesture and at the same time the most gratifying. I always say it costs very little, but it's worth a lot; it only lasts as long as a wink, and yet at times its effect lasts a lifetime. Even the wealthy need it, and they can offer it to the poorest. Without a doubt, it is a gift from God. You can't borrow it, nor buy it, nor steal it; it is a gift. Never forget to smile, even when it seems impossible for you to do it."

Her lips, which were upturned in the sweetest expression, showed me that she also lived what she preached.

"Please follow me."

My old pastor was very pale, but when I stuck my head in the door of his bedroom, he greeted me, lifting up his arms cordially.

"Oh, how I've wanted to see you again!"

"How are you doing?" My voice trembled.

"Well, this body refuses to function as it should," he said as he lightly touched his side. "But I manage to make it get along."

He laughed weakly, and his faint laugh lit up a thousand lamps in my discouragement.

His Bible was resting on top of his chest, well-worn from loving it so much and underlined from all his effort of studying it. The margins were filled with notes, and the edges of the pages were curled.

"It's a real mess," he apologized when he noticed I was looking at it. "Rachel has told me a thousand times that I should buy a new one, but I just can't get rid of this one."

He picked it up with an exquisite sweetness and caressed it with hands covered with skin blemishes, swollen veins, and bones that could be seen through his translucent skin. Yet as those hands moved over the Bible, they did not seem like hands but rather like angel wings.

"It has accompanied me for so long that I can't imagine myself without it."

"There's no doubt you enjoy reading it." I felt a bit guilty at seeing the devotion of this man for his Bible.

"It's my delight. No other book, I assure you"—and he repeated it with determination—"no other book has caused me to grow like this one. Every morning it has a new message for me, and every afternoon I can entertain myself with its stories. Any book can give facts, but this one transforms. There are almost two thousand books in my library that have facts, but this one," he squeezed the Bible against his chest, "this is the only one that has power."

"Do you read the whole thing every year? A little while ago some friends and I were discussing the advantage of reading the Bible every year."

"I'm not sure," he confessed. "And that really doesn't matter to me. I prefer to make sure I read it every day."

"Don't you have responsibilities that prevent you from having time to study it?"

"Don't view the Bible as your workbook. Make it a collection of love letters that God has written to you. Then when you read it, it will cease to be an obligation and turn into sheer delight."

He opened it and thumbed through the pages with his long, thin, trembling fingers, like branches from a vine shoot.

"Look . . ." His index finger was shaking noticeably over the underlined verse. "I made this note the day the Bible gave me an encouraging message in the middle of my defeat. This other note"—he jumped to another page with great ease—"relates to the time when the sacred text became a ladder that was able to lift me up out of the deep valley of discouragement in which I was submerged."

He looked at me with an exquisite and calming tenderness before declaring, "This book is a chest full of treasures and perfect gems for every occasion."

"Certainly, no one can say you don't love your Bible."

"I can assure you it's not because of me."

His devotion was as great as his humility.

"How can I not love it, since it has saved my life so many times?"

"Saved your life?"

"Look," he said as he took his Bible and shook it in front of me with the scant energy that sprung from his body. "This book is the ship that is bringing me to the safest harbor. At times I climbed about this ship absolutely exhausted, but she carried me to the cross. It was there I was reborn. Why are there so few churches where they preach the whole Bible message? Why do so many prefer to tell other stories? There may be more attractive messages, but none more powerful. Many topics may be entertaining, but they don't save. Other issues might astonish, but only the cross can transform us."

He returned the Bible on top of his chest and took my hand in between his hands, looking at me urgently.

"As you develop your ministry, don't focus on what is astonishing but rather on what transforms . . . People don't come to church to be amazed with the eloquence of the one who is preaching; they go there to eat the oldest food and at the same time the most essential—the message of the Word of God. Have you heard about the designer kitchen?"

I shook my head, and he went on to explain it to me. "Plates are neatly garnished, but they only contain two grams of food."

He began to laugh.

"If I go there hungry, I don't want bells and whistles. What I want is food. There are messages that are as empty as they are garnished. Run from them. On the other hand, God has granted me the gift of hearing some anointed preaching . . . so full of the Bible and backed up by the Spirit that when the meeting was over, I could say: 'Today I have eaten.' Don't be a gourmet chef at the altar of the church. Be decisive in the kitchen, and to do that the fundamental ingredients must be the Bible, study, and prayer. Serve good portions of these things and then you can decorate the plate as much as you want. Strive for excellence in the presentation, but make sure, of above all, that it contains nutritious food."

As I watched my old pastor and judged the passion that he felt for his Bible, I couldn't help feeling a lashing in my conscience, remembering a vivid event that took place not long ago.

It had happened while I was traveling in the Metro in Madrid. I was carrying a Bible under my arm. It was a large, black, gilt-edged Bible that I carried to church every Sunday.

Suddenly, a group of boys who were traveling in the same car began to stare at me intently. I knew for sure those boys had realized that what I was carrying under my arm was not a sports magazine but rather a religious book. And I had no doubt, because they began to whisper among themselves and point at me as they laughed.

My reaction was instant. At the first stop, I got off the train and waited for the next one. But I have to confess that I took my jacket off and carefully wrapped the Bible in it so it couldn't be seen. An immense feeling of shame overcame me instantly. I had a mixture of feelings, but those that prevailed were guilt and sadness. The judgment of the gospel that echoed in my mind with the force of thunder was: "For whoever is ashamed of Me and My words . . . of him the Son of Man also will be ashamed . . ." (Mark 8:38). The apostle's admirable boldness was accusing me: "For I am not ashamed of the gospel of Christ, for it is the power of God to salvation" (Romans 1:16).

The train disappeared in the darkness of the tunnel, and I did too. The darkness of guilt filled me completely. Slowly, I reached my hand inside my jacket that was tight against my chest. I closed my fingers firmly around the sacred book and brought it out. Almost instantly, a peace filled me. I opened the Bible and began to read: "Therefore God is not ashamed to be called their God, for He has prepared a city for them" (Hebrews 11:16). I felt that God was smiling at me, pointing at me and saying, *You are My son. I am your Father . . . I am proud of you.* Right then I heard a clear, gentle voice behind me.

"Sir, is that a Bible you are reading?"

I turned around to find blue eyes like two pieces of the sky that were smiling at me with the pure innocence of childhood.

"Yes," I said, a bit surprised. "I'm reading the Bible."

"Me too, sir," said the girl, who then showed me a children's Bible with its cover almost torn from the pages. It was completely deteriorated from being used so much. "Look, sir, this is my favorite passage: 'Let the little children come to Me, and do not forbid them . . .' Jesus was so good! Don't you agree, sir?"

In the silence of that train, the voice of a little girl could be clearly heard, but for me it was a heavenly whisper. Many eyes drilled us with curiosity, but the little girl went on showing me the beautiful things she had read in the Bible.

"Well, my favorite passage," I almost shouted, "is the one that appears in the gospel of John, chapter three, verse sixteen. Do you know it?"

"You bet I do," the little girl shouted with childlike glee.

"Can you explain it to me?"

It was getting dark, but the warmth continued to overwhelm me when I finally left my old pastor's house. Not even the slightest breeze was stirring, and the stillness in that deserted countryside was absolute but delightfully inspiring.

I was not surprised to discover a new red rose that was beginning to open amid its fellow companions. Its petals were fresh, and its perfection and beauty stood out even among the shadows.

The Eighth Monday

What Astonishes and What Transforms

The simple flame of a candle is more effective to fight the darkness than an impressive but ephemeral explosion of firecrackers.

That Monday I arrived a little earlier than normal, and I promised Rachel that my visit would be brief. The last thing I wanted to do was deplete the little strength my old pastor still had.

"Don't you worry," she assured me. "Your visits recharge his batteries, and they are a great encouragement during this difficult time."

When we opened the door of his room, we saw that he was sleeping.

"It's the sedative," Rachel apologized. "The medicines ease

his pain, but they either plunge him into constant sleep or keep him awake."

"Will he mind if I sit near the head of his bed?" I asked his kind wife. "I will read until he wakes up."

For a few seconds after Rachel had left, I watched and listened to my old pastor's peaceful sleeping. Seeing how he was resting brought to mind the image of a courageous soldier who rests right after a battle.

"Sleep and rest," I whispered, knowing that he didn't hear me. "Your life has had purpose, and you have left tracks along the way that others of us desire to follow . . ."

I was startled when I felt my old pastor's stare; he had suddenly opened his eyes.

"You're here. I'm sorry," he apologized. "I spend my day sleeping. I think I bore Rachel so much with my stories that she gives me my pill to make me fall asleep and keep me quiet."

"I don't believe that's the case," I laughed, patting his arm with affection. "It's good for you to rest, and if you want to fall asleep again, I can go and come back another time."

"Absolutely not! Your company makes me feel better. Talking to you makes me learn things."

"Learn things?" I was perplexed at such words from an eighty-three-year-old wise man to a novice like me. I thought about how inspiring humility is.

"You know," I said to him, "I have not stopped thinking about the words you said to me last Monday. 'Don't focus on what astonishes, but rather what transforms.' I've thought a lot about your advice, and I'm convinced that it contains an important principle."

"Son"—the expression on my old pastor's face left no doubt about what was troubling him—"I fear that too many churches have backed away from their solemn responsibilities in the face of pressure for what is 'in style.' They have changed the focus of their ministries and directed their efforts to satisfying human expectations rather than divine ones. What happens at times is that what should be a service of worship to God becomes a service to worship emotions. They transform the simple and powerful act of worship into a spectacle to show off abilities and stir up feelings, which succeeds in amazing the people with new electronic gadgets and special effects."

My old pastor waited in silence to make sure I was following what he was saying.

"I understand," I nodded. "It's about churches that are more worried about gathering the 'faithful' than invoking God's presence.

"But I wouldn't call them 'faithful,' because they will leave as soon as they hear of a more attractive program. Something like that is what happens, and the consequences are evident: churches overflowing with believers who are jumping and shaking to the rhythm of the music like epileptics having a seizure. They shout and even cry, overwhelmed by a show more electronic than spiritual, but then they leave their churches and go out into society without making any difference . . . no difference at all."

He looked at me, scrutinizing the reaction that his words had caused in me.

"Please understand me. I have nothing against good music or cutting-edge technology. I can appreciate a church being contemporary and relevant in its worship and preaching. I understand that in order to reach society in the twenty-first century, we can't use nineteenth-century methods. But I do believe that true worship of God should cause people to change. Man-made worship is something else. Too many churches open their doors once the service is over and send out a group into the world that are astonished by the 'show,' but not changed one iota. Astonished, but not transformed. They're megachurches in numbers, but microchurches in quality."

I agreed with my old pastor's message, which encouraged him to go on.

"Our questions are often: How many? How many raised their hands in response to the call? How many were in attendance? How many sermons have we preached? How many churches have we started?"

His expression was evocative, and there was conviction in his words.

"God's questions are: Who? and How? Who raised their hands? Who preached the sermon? What's the person's life like who went out and did it? What's the church like that we've started? Who is serving in it? What are the lives like of those who have surrendered to Me?"

He closed his eyes and kept them closed for so long that I thought he had fallen asleep again, but then he opened them and asked me, "Would you be so kind as to hand me that wooden box that's on the chest of drawers?"

I handed it to him, and he placed it on his legs, without opening it, while he explained, "Rachel and I used to spend our summers in a small fishing village on the Alicante coastland. It's a peaceful place that still maintains the traditions of the fishermen from years ago. We loved going down to the harbor in the late afternoon to watch the ships come in that had been out working since early in the morning. A number of times we went to the traditional fish market, where the different businesses and restaurant owners would bid to take home the best fish at the best price. But one of the most special times of our vacations happened one night in July. It was the day they lit up what they called 'the castle of fireworks' on the beach. The same event happened each year. When it would start to get dark, the crowd would draw close to the beach to get as close to the sea as possible. At midnight, they would turn off the lights on the boardwalk near the water, and everything would be plunged in total darkness. Suddenly, the first firework would streak up into the air and explode high above, turning into a million flashes of different colors. That was just the beginning. From that moment the night sky became a canvas on which the most beautiful pictures of light were painted with fire and gunpowder. For the next fifteen minutes the sky was filled with the sound of explosions, mixed with exclamations of admiration and amazement from those of us who had come to see that impressive pyrotechnical demonstration. Everything had been planned to achieve fifteen minutes of amazement and admiration. The last explosions, which made the ground shake where we were seated, announced that the show was over, and then silence returned along with the darkness."

"That must have been beautiful," I replied. "You've described it with such detail that I can almost see the lights in the sky and hear the sound of the explosions."

"In fact it was," my old pastor admitted. "It really was beautiful, but after that night each year I would do the same thing: I'd get up early the next morning and walk on the same beach where only hours before we had stood with our mouths open in amazement, and you know what I would find?"

Without waiting for my answer, he opened up the box on his lap and from the inside took out pieces of burned cardboard, wires, and burned matches.

"This is what was scattered on the sand."

He held it up, and I noticed that his hands had gotten dirty with the leftover powder and burned cardboard.

"They're the broken pieces of those fireworks that left us all wonderstruck. The fuses and wires that made up a short-lived show." He looked at me meaningfully. "Fifteen minutes of glory, and then burned cardboard."

I smiled at how didactic his analogy was.

"It could cause us to laugh if it wasn't so sad, my son. These burned pieces of cardboard remind me of too many people who were amazing for a short time but then ended up as burned-up cinders. Charismatic people, lofty preachers, men and women who sing like angels or make music worthy of the stars . . . but after being amazing, they disappeared or blackened with soot those who came looking for more from them. Yes"—he repeated with a growing tone of sadness—"there are too many who from a distance amaze people, but up close they only tarnish people."

My old pastor once again stuck his hand inside the wooden box, and this time he took out a simple white candle.

"Would you turn the light off, please?"

I flicked the switch, and the room went dark. My old pastor lit a match and lit the candle with it, whose flame stood straight up.

"This is better," he said. "Do you see it? This little flame . . . this orange point that can't even be seen during the day becomes a beacon for seafarers so they can make course corrections when it's dark out. Can you appreciate how this simple light has overcome the darkness? It will not amaze anyone, but it will be able to push back the darkness. This candle represents the hundreds of men and women who by simple, subtle, and inconspicuous acts bring about change and turn on lights in their community. Ask God for the gift of having many of this kind of people in your church."

"Remarkable," I whispered, impressed. "It's a powerful illustration."

"Did you know that the light from a candle can be seen seventeen miles away?"

He wisely remained quiet so I could take in how convincing that message was, and then he added, "Only one thing is necessary: darkness."

He looked at me intently.

"Son, there is enough darkness around that we need a real army of simple candles. Tiny flames will bring about the most powerful changes. I don't doubt for a minute that Albert Einstein was truly a wise man. He not only contributed to the advance of science, but he also had a deeper wisdom. On one occasion he said, "'Instead of being a successful man, seek to be a man of value. The rest will come naturally.'" Don't focus on what astonishes, but rather what transforms. Don't let yourself be impressed by fireworks that surprise people for fifteen minutes and then leave them tarnished. Look for something deeper. Don't make it your goal to amaze your audience. Don't rest until you are sure that your ministry crosses the frontier of the soul and touches the spirit, the place where change is accomplished."

He blew on the candle's flame, and it went out. I flicked the switch to turn on the light.

My old pastor handed me the box. Taking it, I put it back on the chest of drawers. When I turned around, I discovered the old man had fallen asleep.

He was breathing calmly, exhaling a supernatural peace.

He was sleeping, but his message had woken me up.

I left slowly, trying not to disturb my old pastor's rest. I didn't even see Rachel as I headed for the door. And soon after I found myself kneeling next to the rosebush.

A tiny rose was about to open. It was the eighth red flower that had bloomed from that rose bush. Its fragrance wasn't even noticeable, but it displayed the purity of its simplicity in the night.

Beneath the sky, which was completely dark, I lifted a prayer heavenward: "That's just how I want to be, Lord, a simple instrument fulfilling an eternal purpose. The most useless instrument, but in the most useful hands: Your hands."

The Ninth Monday

It's Not How You Start
but How You Finish

Faithfulness is shown by staying put. The trees whose wood is most sought after grow on the most rugged slopes of the mountain.

T he cross seems heavy at times, doesn't it?"

In asking him the question, I knew I was standing in front of a man who carried his cross with admirable faithfulness.

"Perseverance is fundamental," he clarified. "'Deny yourself,' Jesus said, 'and take up your cross every day.' There are 'spring' Christians who disappear in the winter. They're like the birds that constantly migrate in search of warmer climate. An authentic Christian is characterized by faithfulness. Have you heard of Francis Nichol?"

"Never," I confessed.

117

"I don't know much about him either, except a phrase that is attributed to him, and a while back it left me pensive: 'When you finally fully understand the root of the word *success*, you discover that it means 'keep going forward.''" I think the picture it's trying to paint is one of a tree that endures bad weather, but it remains there, where it was planted."

"At times," I risked saying, "the wind can blow so hard that it threatens to uproot us."

"Far from it," he countered determinedly. "The storm serves to strengthen us. Did you know that logging companies not only have people who cut down trees but also people who specialize in reforestation? They know where to plant a tree so its wood has a better quality. When they go out to reforest a mountain, they scan over its slopes until they find what they call stress factors."

"Stress factors?"

"Yes, the stress factors are the areas on the mountain more exposed to winds and storms. Right there, where the stress factors are the most obvious, is where they plant the trees. From day one these little trees understand the cruelty of winter and the rigors of the summer. When strong storms come along, they know that their only option to survive is to sink down their roots deeper. And in times of extreme drought, they sink those roots even farther down to find subterranean springs. During this difficult process their trunks get harder. Of course not all survive, but those that do will have better wood . . . the most desired and sought after."

"Then there's no doubt that suffering always strengthens us when the wind isn't so strong as to knock us over."

"That's how it is with trees, but not with us," my old pastor observed. "That's why we have faith. Anxiety is able to keep us awake all night, but faith is a marvelous pillow. The most important thing is not starting the race, but rather the unwavering determination to reach the finish line. Let me tell you a story."

It was his introduction phrase, so I got ready to listen to another one of his interesting tales.

There's a little anecdote of Leonardo da Vinci, the great painter, sculptor, and inventor, about his painting The Last Supper, *one of the most copied and sold works of art in all of history. It took da Vinci twenty years to finish, since it was so difficult at that time to find people who could pose as models. In fact, he had problems in starting the painting because he couldn't find a model who could represent Jesus, someone who could reflect in his face purity, nobility, and the loveliest feelings. Also, the model needed to possess extraordinary manly beauty. Finally, he found a young man with these characteristics, and it was the first figure of the picture he painted.*

Later, he went looking for the twelve apostles, whom he painted together, leaving Judas Iscariot's spot open, since he couldn't find a suitable model. It had to be a person of mature age who had a face with the traces of betrayal and greed. That is why the painting remained unfinished for a long time, until they told him of a terrible criminal who had been taken prisoner. Da Vinci went to see him, and he was exactly the Judas he wanted to finish his work. So he asked the mayor to allow the prisoner to pose for him. The mayor, knowing the master's fame, gladly accepted and

*ordered that the prisoner be taken to the painter's studio, chained
and accompanied by two guards.*

*During all that time, the prisoner showed no signs of emotion for having been chosen as a model, but remained completely
quiet and distant. Finally, when da Vinci was satisfied with the
result, he called the prisoner over and showed him the painting.
When the prisoner saw it, he was greatly impressed and fell to
his knees, crying. Surprised, da Vinci asked why he was crying,
to which the prisoner responded: "Master da Vinci, don't you
remember me?"*

*After looking at him carefully, Da Vinci answered him, "No,
I have never seen you."*

*Crying and asking for forgiveness from God, the prisoner
said to him, "Master, I am the young man you chose nineteen
years ago to represent Jesus in this same painting."*[1]

My old pastor was tired by the time he had finished his story.
Without saying anything to me, he closed his eyes, and I thought
he was sleeping.

I slowly got up to leave the room and let him rest, but when I
put my hand on the doorknob, I heard him calling me. With his
hand, he was making signs for me to come close.

"Travel on the road of the cross until the end," he told me.
His eyes had a layer of water covering them, on which a smile was
cradled. "Don't give up. The cross has its price . . . but there is
nothing more beautiful, or more worthy of embracing."

The night was like a dark, warm cloak when I left the house.
The moon had sketched my shadow, and beneath its aura I made

the firm decision that I had to write all of this in a memory journal—the journal that you are reading right now.

I stopped once again in front of the rosebush planted in that large tub. The white roses were still standing straight up, and among them, the light night breeze was swaying the red ones from the previous Monday, which were still fresh and moist. To their side, a new one was beginning to open. Its few petals, though still in a tight bud, were a purple color that almost bordered on black.

I stood there, next to the door, and looked up at the sky, at the small bits of night that wrapped around the stars.

"God is in love with us," my old pastor had told me. "Nature offers us a thousand gifts that demonstrate the love God has for us."

The Tenth Monday

The Minutes That Make
Life Profitable

*If you want to have a decisive influence, sit at the feet of Christ
each day, and then tell the world what you have seen.*

"Y ou should come by," Rachel told me over the phone, reject-
ing my excuses. "Really, you won't bother him. I know the
time he spends with you rejuvenates him."

I accepted the flattery, but went over determined to stay only
a short while and not tire my old pastor.

October had come in without clouds or cold; just a few
tugs of soft fog, which as it vanished, raised the sky, painting
it blue. Now the afternoon was pleasant, and everything was
at rest around the house. The trees that surrounded the house,
whose leaves had taken on a yellow hue or dark rust throughout
September, were now shedding their dead skin, which shriveled

up and covered the ground with yellow, and then was carried away by the wind in November.

I stared for a few seconds at the leaves that were crunching under my feet.

Will that be the only thing November's wind carries away? I shivered as I thought about my old pastor.

I found him in bed, as I expected. He was even thinner but smiling as usual.

"I will bring coffee right away," Rachel announced. "Would you like some cookies?"

I shook my head no, though my stomach reminded me that I hadn't eaten since morning. But I didn't want to make work for Rachel. She already had enough on her plate.

It's possible that my old pastor had read my thoughts, or perhaps he had heard my stomach growl, because he asked his wife, "Bring him some of those cookies you have baked."

He made his request with a voice weaker than normal and, looking at me, added, "You'll see that you haven't tasted anything better in your life."

She smiled at him, grateful and timid at the same time, while a slight blush colored her cheeks.

Rachel came back shortly with steaming coffee and a tray of cookies.

"Try them, try them," my old pastor said with almost child-like insistence.

"Yum. They are delicious!" I closed my eyes with the next bite. "You're right. They're exquisite."

"What did I tell you?" He made an attempt to sit up to emphasize his words. "She is an extraordinary cook."

I loved that ability to get excited about something so simple even in the midst of his terrible sickness. His expression made me remember the accurate reflection that I heard long ago: "Many people lose the simple joys while they are waiting for great happiness. Perhaps it is better to enjoy collecting seashells than to be born a millionaire."[1] What a great truth that thought contained!

Rachel leaned over and kissed her husband's lips tenderly.

"You exaggerate too much," she told him as she caressed his cheek.

Before Rachel withdrew her hand, my old pastor took it and kissed it.

"I don't exaggerate at all, Rachel. I'm proud of you."

I felt like an intruder invading his personal space, but I thoroughly enjoyed the tender scene. I had no doubt that this scene I was observing had a lot to do with our latest reflections: serving others and denying ourselves. It was what this long-married couple had done all their lives and what they were doing now for each other.

Right there in front of me were two heroes of the cross. They both had their particular pains, but they had decided to look past them to pour out their love on the other.

When Rachel left, my pastor sat up with difficulty and asked me to give him an envelope from the first drawer in the dresser.

I handed it to him, and he pulled out a paper that had turned yellow over the years.

"Look," he said as he unfolded the paper and handed it to me. "It's a short letter I wrote to a veteran pastor when as a young, fearful, and inexperienced young man I accepted the pastorate of the church you so well know."

The sheet of paper had two fold marks, and the ink was faded but still legible. I could tell that the letter had been written with the same fountain pen he had used to write every one of his sermons.

With a look I asked for permission to read it, and with a gesture of his hand he encouraged me to begin reading.

> *Dear Pastor Rodriguez:*
>
> *Please forgive my boldness in writing to you and robbing a few minutes of your valuable time. It's my need of advice that has caused me to write you.*
>
> *I have just been ordained as a pastor of a small church, and I feel that the responsibility is too much for me. I'm facing this sublime challenge with a mixture of feelings, of which fear and anxiety are the strongest.*
>
> *On one hand, I feel privileged to serve our God, but on the other hand, I'm overwhelmed by fear because I don't know how to do it. I fear that I will fail at this high calling, and so I'm begging you for some advice that will help me to effectively and confidently begin this extraordinary journey.*
>
> *Sincerely grateful, I greet you with affection and admiration.*

I looked at my old pastor, and he, aware that I had understood the meaning of his story, stared at me intently for a moment. I tried to picture him as the naive young man who decades ago had written that request for help, but I couldn't.

Had it been just the years that had transformed a frightened young man into a strong servant and anointed him with such unquestionable authority?

I couldn't stop looking at his face, which was deeply lined with wrinkles that seemed like battle scars to me, and I decided no, the years of his life were not responsible for that change. It wasn't the years of his life but rather the life he had poured into those years.

"Now you understand," he said, taking the sheet of paper and folding it up again. "I also had my fears. A lot of them, and some were very big ones."

"Did you ever receive an answer?" I asked with impatient interest.

"Here it is."

The sheet of paper he handed me now was as old as the first one. When I unfolded it, I noticed that it was dated twenty days after the first one.

> *Dear Colleague:*
>
> *I appreciate and thank you for the trust that was evident in your question. Let me say that I congratulate you for accepting the challenge of the pastorate. It is a risk, I do not doubt, but at the same time it entails a high privilege.*
>
> *You ask my advice, and I feel inadequate to give it to you. I, too, am learning, despite the fact that three weeks ago I celebrated my seventy-fifth birthday.*
>
> *It's not advice I'm going to share with you, but a key that has worked for me.*
>
> *The first thing I did each morning, the first activity that I gave myself to, was to kneel at the feet of Christ and contemplate Him in worship. That vision has transformed my life.*

It may seem simple, but I wouldn't trade it for anything. To surrender myself to intimacy with Jesus during the first minutes of the day has been the driving force of my life and ministry.

Sitting at His feet, I have admired Him, and He has re-created me in His presence . . . the rest came naturally.

When He speaks, His voice transforms me; then all I have to do is reproduce His words. When He looks at me, His love inspires me and at the same time grants me His authority.

Dear colleague. If you are asking for my advice, it would be this: carefully read this phrase because it contains the essence of fifty years of service: Sit every day at the feet of Christ, and then tell the world what you have seen.

Affectionately in Him,

For almost a whole minute I stared at the sheet of paper.

"Sit every day at the feet of Christ, and then tell the world what you have seen," I said finally without raising my eyes from the letter, allowing the profoundness of that statement to soak in.

"I have put that into practice every day," he added. "I worked as if everything depended on me, and I prayed as if everything depended on God. I have found no other place more delightful than sitting next to Jesus. That is the secret for living and serving even in the midst of difficulty."

I pondered what he said as I listened to him.

I didn't know how to respond, nor was he waiting for an answer. He fixed his eyes on me and smiled, and every crease on his face lit up. Looking at him, I remembered the phrase that someone had told me long ago: "You can trust the person who turns beautiful when they smile."

"Fall in love with God!" he told me with authority but without losing his tenderness. "He is absolutely in love with us. There are so many ways He demonstrates it: the growing light of dawn, the dimming light at twilight. The delicious mix of colors in nature. The symphony that birds create in any forest. We are surrounded by a thousand gifts from a God in love with us. Loving Him should be our first priority and the only and sufficient motivation to serve Him. Look . . . if we do not serve out of love, we will end up giving up on serving. There is not enough human energy to resist the battering of serving your whole life. Only love will provide us the necessary strength to travel this road."

"Love Him," I agreed. "I understand, but how can I love Him more?"

"By knowing Him better."

I was surprised by his instant answer.

"He must be the center of your life and the heart of your ministry," my wise pastor continued. "As for me, the more I know Him, the more I love Him. Just seek Him, prove Him, know Him . . . and loving Him will be a logical outcome. It won't be hard for you. On the contrary, after seeing His smile, it will be impossible for you not to."

"I assure you that I will strive with all my strength to become so in love with God as you are," I told him in the way of a formal promise. I noticed the moisture of unexpected tears in my eyes that threatened to spill out.

"Son, you will not have to strive to fall in love with Him. Simply make room for Him in your daily life. His presence will become so natural for you, and the time will come when you won't be able to live without it."

He reached his hand up to my face and brushed away the tear that was running down my cheek. He added, "Simply live with God. The rest will happen by itself, and that will take care of all your worries. A long time ago I came to a very logical conviction: Why should I worry? It's not my responsibility to think about myself. My responsibility is to think about God. It's God's responsibility to think about me."

I looked at him, amazed at the amount of wisdom contained in such simplicity.

"The last phrase isn't mine," he admitted. "It was a truth spoken by Simone Weil, but I have adopted it as a motto for my life."

As I hugged him for a long time during our good-bye, I had the feeling of holding within my arms an extremely fragile but incredibly strong person.

I remembered the words with which a historian had described Abraham Lincoln: "a man of steel and at the same time one of velvet."[2] That same description equally applied to this servant whom I held in my arms.

"Sit at the feet of Christ," he insisted as he pulled away from my hug. "The world will be amazed when you tell them what you have seen."

As I left his room, I was convinced that his deteriorating body was shining with a supernatural splendor. A light was shining on the inside of him that made him glow.

Night was beginning to fall when I left the house. It wouldn't be long before the moon would rise in the sky and the gardenia flowers would begin to stir up their cloying and warm aromas, but the red rose was still in its place, swaying in the wind, in precise timing, with its budding petals.

When Rachel closed the door, I did not resist the impulse to kneel down in front of the rosebush, nor did I suppress the prayer that rose to my lips: "Help me, God, to live leaning next to Your heart so that my heartbeat is in step with Yours. May Your look be my breath, and may I prefer You above anyone else. May Your voice be my delight, and may I stop listening to my own torturing voice. I want to spend a long time contemplating You so I can describe to the world what true beauty is."

The Eleventh Monday

Scars

The true secret of happiness is not in always doing what you want to do, but in always wanting to do what you do.

The next Monday came, and I went with hope to the place of quietude where my pastor had built his refuge.

The days were becoming shorter, and although it had been cold during the week, today the air was warm.

Contrary to my prediction, he opened the door that day. After a hug filled with affection in mammoth proportions but with minimal traces of strength, he walked in front of me very slowly, as if he were sliding along the floor. Something told me that his days were coming to an end, like the hours of summer light that fall had swallowed up.

The time of his death that the doctors had forecast had already come and gone, but his symptoms shouted with cruel eloquence that the prognosis would surely come to pass. And yet that did not seem to bother him. He was smiling even more. He always was smiling, as if the imminent reunion with his Beloved was renewing his hope.

He turned around to make sure I was following him, and a sweet expression softened his face, lending him a curious child-like appearance.

We crossed through the kitchen and stopped next to the table on the porch, where he let himself sit down on a chair.

"Let's soak up these last rays of sun. There is nothing like the first pinch of sun on one's face when it's cold outside."

He smiled again, reminding me of a happy child.

"This temperature is marvelous."

He pointed me to the chair in front of him.

"You know, son?"—which is what he called me all the time— "Today I felt loved by God."

I remained quiet, enjoying the tone of love that stamped his words.

"He loves us so much. We do not deserve it, but He loves us beyond measure."

"You're right," I agreed timidly.

"Would you let me tell you a story?"

"Please do . . ."

And so he began:

On a hot summer day, a little boy decided to go swimming in the lake behind his house. He went running out the back door, jumped into the water, and was happily swimming. He did not realize that a crocodile was approaching.

His mother, from the house, was looking out the window and saw with horror what was happening. She instantly ran toward her son, shouting at him as loud as she could. Hearing her, the little boy became frightened and turned around and swam toward his mother, but it was too late. From the dock, the mother grabbed the little boy by his arms just as the crocodile bit down on his little legs. The woman pulled on the boy's arms with all her strength. The crocodile was much stronger, but the mother was much more passionate, and her love gave her supernatural strength.

A man who heard the screams hurried over to where they were with a pistol and shot the crocodile several times. The little boy survived, and although his legs suffered a lot and he underwent several surgeries, he still was able to walk. After he had come through the trauma, a newspaperman asked if he could see the scars on his legs. The boy lifted the bedspread and showed them to him. Seeing the worried look on the newspaperman's face, the boy, with great pride, took off his T-shirt and, pointing to the scars on his arms, said, "The scars you need to see are these. The ones that my mother's fingernails left holding on tight so the crocodile wouldn't swallow me. I have these scars because my mother wouldn't let go for a moment, and she saved my life."[1]

My old pastor closed his eyes with emotion.

"Life inflicts wounds on us at times," he whispered, "but when a scar is causing you pain, focus on the real scars, those that were inflicted on the cross. He did not give up on forgiving us, and the nails that pierced Him are an anchor for us so the sea does not swallow us up. That is grace, my son, the unmerited gift of His love."

His message dripped with devotion, and the passion that he filled his words with moved me to tears. There, in front of me, was a man who was almost at the end, but he was regaining all his fervor as he meditated on the love of God.

"'I only know two types of reasonable people,'" he said. "'Those who love God with all their heart because they know Him, and those who are looking for Him with all their heart because they don't know Him.'"

He had just quoted Blaise Pascal, the French scientist who demonstrated a genuine faith throughout his life.

"And never forget that the cross leaves scars," he warned me. "Listen, my son, when we make the decision to carry our cross, we are assuming the risk of suffering. But I assure you, it is worth even suffering. It is even worth dying for the love of the One who suffered so much for us. On the other hand, the scars of whoever serves God are authentic credentials for the ministry. Because, you want to serve God, right?"

He looked at me intently, almost trying to read my answer in my eyes rather than hearing it from my lips.

I waited a few seconds to answer. A holy silence settled on the porch. His eyes continued to scrutinize mine, until finally I spoke.

"The first Monday that I came to your house, I was determined to give up. I felt that the ministry just wasn't for me. The days we have shared together . . . the teaching and the example that you've given me have caused me to know with certainty right now that I will never be happy if I'm not serving God."

A large tear slowly slipped out from the old man's eye, coursed down the side of his nose, moistened his lips, and then fell on his hand resting on his lap. Though his health was deteriorating, his sensitivity was increasing.

With a voice that cracked with emotion, he said, "The secret of happiness is not in always doing what you want to do, but in always wanting to do what you are doing. I'm sure that Mary and you love God and love His work. Your scars show that. Continue loving . . . continue serving . . . Be concerned with the things of God, and don't doubt for a moment that He will take care of you."

He stopped for a moment and stared at me again.

"I have never confessed it openly," he said, and his expression held a hint of mischief. "But all my life I have been passionate about soccer. One of my favorite players, perhaps because of his calmness or for his self-control when under pressure, was Vicente del Bosque. He was the one who picked the team from Spain that won the 2010 World Cup. Asked about his strategy, he responded that his philosophy included *eliminating limiting beliefs*, which meant helping each member of the team to do the best he knew how to do and to execute it as perfectly as possible."

I nodded as I was thinking. Now he was looking at me so intently that it made me shiver.

"Dream big dreams, and you will achieve great things, but make sure to dream using God's heart as a pillow. Don't live in the past. Good memories will lull you to sleep. Great projects will wake you up. There are too many people who are tired, and that's why they live their lives asleep. But others have a dream, and that's why they live their lives awake. Try to get an education in the general sciences, and above all in the Bible, but don't forget that knowledge is just an idling motor. What makes it move is attitude."

He stood up, indicating the meeting was over. In fact, he accompanied me to the door, with short steps as he limped along, but with that fire of love that filled every expression and word, which all the more made him seem like a human torch to me.

He stopped before reaching the door, and I stood by his side. Then he said:

> *Three men were working on building a building. An observer, of those that abound with every job, drew near and asked them, "What are you doing?"*
>
> *The first man, who was loud and lazy, responded without even looking at him, "I'm here laying bricks."*
>
> *The second man, lifting his head and stopping what he was doing for a moment, said, "I'm building a wall."*
>
> *The third man, happy about his work, with a gleam of determination in his look and with a voice of triumph, said, "We're building a church for my town."*

His face broke into a smile, then putting his hand on my shoulder, he asked me, "Do you know what motivation is?"

He didn't give me time to answer. His hand tightened a little on my shoulder as he went on to explain: "Motivation is what mobilizes a person to perform an activity. It's what moves us to undertake something with hope and makes us carry it out as we overcome obstacles that arise, by applying the necessary effort."

He focused his eyes on mine, and that look added enormous authority to his words: "You are not piling bricks or even building a wall. You are building a church . . . the church of Christ.

There is nothing more worthy to invest your life in. Do it with joy. It's worth even suffering. It's worth even dying for. You have been chosen. You are a privileged man. Live close to God, and then life itself will continually surprise you with opportunities you've never dreamed about." He became quiet for a moment before insisting, "With God a human being can fly, even though he doesn't have wings. How could you not attain what you set your mind to?"

Leaning on me, he continued his way to the door. This little time of talking while we were standing there had left him with almost no strength.

Night was falling when I left the house.

I was trembling with emotion. The sensitivity of my old pastor was contagious, and I cried as I worshipped God.

One tear, large and round like a huge raindrop, fell onto the petals of the new red rose that had just opened and remained there, shining like a pearl when a moonbeam kissed it.

The Twelfth Monday

Smoke in the Chimney

Don't be a servant with an open day planner and a closed Bible. Never let your day planner suffocate your Bible.

D uring my next visit, Rachel didn't leave our side for one instant. It was as if she knew that my pastor didn't have much more time, and she didn't want to waste even one minute.

Yet it wasn't compassion that moved her to protect him but rather the true love that she felt for him. I believe she felt protected sitting next to her husband's fragile body.

"Please come in," my old pastor said to me when I knocked on the door of his room and stuck my head in. "Oh, how I've wanted to see you again!"

His politeness was always the same, but his strength wasn't. He greeted me from his bed, stretching his arms toward me, but without sitting up. Because of how pale he looked, his face almost blended in with the pillow.

"How are you doing today?"

I wanted to seem normal, but the tremor in my voice gave it away.

"Well, as long as we don't go into detail . . ." he joked.

As usual, his open Bible lay on top of his chest. He never left it out of his sight. Not for one instant.

"You know? I spent the night meditating on a story," he said.

"And why don't you spend your nights sleeping," I scolded him, using my best smile.

He laughed, thanking me for my reproof.

"I wish I could!" he responded, shrugging his shoulders. Then he added, "But what would you like me to do? For even sleep escapes this old man. As I was saying, I spent the night remembering a story."

"He sure did," Rachel said as she affectionately patted her husband's wrinkled hand. Then holding it wrapped in her hands, she added, "He woke me up to tell it to me, and this morning he's asked me ten times already when you were coming."

The old man smiled tenderly at his wife, and then fixed his gaze on me.

"You won't be bothered if this old sick man bores you with another one of his stories?"

"Absolutely not!" I told him as I lightly squeezed his weak, bony arm with my hand. "And don't call yourself sick. I've seen very few people with as much life as you have."

"The church you are serving in is a hundred years old. Did you know that?"

"Yes," I answered. "I know that the church has a long history."

"Good."

He sat up with great difficulty, so we placed the pillows behind his back so he would be more comfortable. After that he went on with his story: "When Rachel and I graduated from seminary, we went to that town. We were newlyweds, and that was going to be my first church, and the one that I would pastor for the rest of my life."

A slight cough caused him to stop. He moved his hand to his chest, and his expression showed pain.

Worried, I asked him, "Are you tired? If you want, we can continue another day."

"No," he said, "let me tell you the story."

Rachel gave him a glass of water, and after taking a sip, he recovered fast. "When we got to the town, we were greeted by a deacon who took us around in his car and showed us the little village and the church. Then he took us to the parish home, and along the way we had an interesting talk.

"'This church,' said the deacon with evident pride, 'has a long history. Many good pastors have passed through here . . . but we have had some bad ones.'"[1]

My old pastor turned toward me and blessed me with a beautiful smile as he commented: "When the deacon made that statement, I felt Rachel's elbow in my ribs, as if to say, *Listen up, here comes a lesson.* 'What do you expect from a pastor?' I asked him, fearing that his answer would include a string of titles and academic merits.

"'That he gets up early.'

"His answer was as brief as it was final, and unexpected as well. 'That he doesn't sleep in late,' insisted the deacon.

"'And how are you going to know if your pastor gets up early or not?'

"'Do you see that chimney?' he asked me. Then without awaiting my answer, he added, 'Even though it's early, if there's smoke there, that means those who are at home are up. Do you see that other house? They've already gotten up to light a fire in the home. Look,' he said to me as he pointed in another direction. 'That's the parish home, but there's no smoke in the chimney.'

"The deacon then explained his curious conclusion: 'I go by here early every morning on my way to work, and when I do, I want to see smoke in my pastor's chimney. That tells me that he's up, praying for every one of us and preparing spiritual food for us. That's what we expect from our pastor: that he get up early to seek God.'"

The old man had closed his eyes, remembering the story of the beginning of his ministry.

Rachel delicately wiped the corners of his lips with a handkerchief. Without opening his eyes, he continued with his story: "So each day I would get up early, and the first thing I would do was build a fire in the chimney. Then I would get down on my knees in prayer, lifting each one of them in my prayers and worshipping God. Often, while I was still on my knees, I would read His Word and inquire into His mysteries. That way I would feel refreshed and renewed."

He laughed as he added, "The second result was that every Sunday I would see all the deacons sitting in the first row smiling and content. They all knew that their pastor was getting up early."

"That's an interesting story," I said to him, "and it contains a great truth."

"There on my knees I would receive food for my church."

He smiled with a delightful sweetness.

"That is important, right?"

He ignored my question, but what he told me afterward answered it: "There are other more popular emphases, but less evangelical. The cross has enemies. There are pulpits where it is absent, and altars where other styles are used. There are messages that entertain but do not transform. There are services that supposedly are directed toward God, but He doesn't show up. The gospel and the cross are missing, and they are nothing more but shows that turn the altar into a stage. They amaze but they don't transform . . . They entertain, but they don't save."

I never let my old pastor know that some of the things he was telling me he had already told me previously, because it would only interrupt him. And besides, among the things he had already said were many new things that I wanted to know.

"So as you got up early to light the fire in the chimney and seek God, He would show you the message you were supposed to share, is that it?"

My old pastor took on a serious expression, almost one of worry. He once again focused his intense gaze on me to concentrate on the second part of the story: "Yes. All that happened as I sought Him. But the ministry began to grow as well as my influence, which now was not limited to our small church. My responsibilities that absorbed me and demanded my time only increased. Before I knew it, I still was getting up early to light the chimney, but I stopped kneeling down for prayer."

He acknowledged his failure with the shaking of his head, and his voice was muffled, as if covered with a shawl of sadness.

"I didn't kneel down to pray, nor did I open my Bible. What I opened now was my day planner, which was filling up with commitments and obligations. The first task of the morning stopped being the choice of sacred passages to delight myself in, and instead I spent that time choosing urgent matters to give myself to each day."

He breathed deeply before adding: "I made the mistake many pastors do: confusing the urgent with the important. My day planner was taking the place of my Bible. I had succeeded in turning myself into an executive of an open day planner and a closed Bible. My influence was growing, but my spiritual life was shrinking. There was smoke in the chimney, but there was no fire in my heart."

"Smoke in the chimney, but no fire in my heart," I repeated the sentence, realizing the profoundness it contained.

"That's right."

While one of his hands was still wrapped between his wife's hands, he put the other one on my arm, and I covered it with mine.

"I kept on giving advice because my brain was functioning, but that advice lacked the freshness of heaven. I spoke from the pulpit like one who has to say something, not like someone who has something to say."

He stopped for an instant to ask me: "Do you understand the difference?"

There was urgency in his words.

"Do you understand that having to say something is not the same as having something to say?"

"There's a huge difference between the one and the other," I agreed.

"Birds chirp, frogs croak, dogs bark, humans speak, and those who are in fellowship with God speak and express eternal truths. My message had human wisdom, but it lacked divine freshness. It didn't have spiritual influence. I showed off theoretical knowledge of Christ, but He and His cross were missing."

"It must have been hard," I said, though surprised at my pastor's frankness.

"It was, and not just for me, but it was hard for the congregation I was pastoring. My words no longer brought the breeze of heaven near. Instead, those words had such an earthy taste to them that they grated against the heart."

A coughing spell interrupted his story, but he made signs with his hands that everything was okay, and he soon started with his message again.

"One day I couldn't stand it anymore. I felt so empty that I decided to go out to the countryside to seek God. I left my day planner at home and all the worries and obligations that filled my mind. I only took my Bible and the deep dissatisfaction that I felt. There, leaning against a tree, I spoke with God and opened up my heart to Him. I begged Him to rekindle the flame of His presence in me. I didn't want to dry up and turn the church into a desert."

My old pastor closed his eyes once again at this point in the story. After a few seconds of silence, he went on with his confession.

"God was faithful. He always is, and He renewed me. My desire to seek Him resurfaced, and I felt a voracious hunger for His Word come to life again. The next morning I lit a fire in the chimney, and as I knelt on my knees, I sensed that my heart was on fire as well. There wasn't just smoke in the chimney, but my inner being was also on fire. Never again was my Bible closed because of my day planner. Never again did planning my day take the place of worship."

I was definitely in the presence of a man in love with God, the cross, and the Bible. And that love was extraordinarily contagious.

I took his Bible and paged through it. Those pages, worn and curled on the edges, exuded profound and intimate experiences.

"Never hide the Bible." He was looking at me imploringly as he insisted, "Never suffocate your Bible with your agenda . . . never do it."

I put my hand on his shoulder and gently squeezed, grateful for the personal confessions he had offered me.

I looked at that emaciated face with no color, and those arms whose bones protruded beneath the skin with shocking insolence; at the same time, I noticed the anointing and wisdom that flowed from his words, and I remembered an old reflection that someone had told me one day: "Some birds can't be caged; their feathers are too beautiful to be caged up, and their songs must flow in the freedom of the forests."

And that's how my old pastor was. Sickness could make him its target, but not its prisoner. Even though a hundred shackles of pain might want to hold him down, he continued to soar up through unfathomable skies.

Only Rachel accompanied me to the door.

The sky had taken on the purple shades of twilight. Confused perhaps by the warm temperature that seemed like that of summer nights, bats dizzyingly flitted through the sky in a pattern that left mysterious signs in the air.

I looked for the rosebush, convinced that today the same miracle would have happened. There it was, intact, with its white roses that competed in beauty with the fresh red roses that had bloomed.

And there was one more.

Another crimson rose was begging to open.

I was surprised to discover that the arrangement of the red flowers formed the exact shape of a cross.

Night had fallen, and beneath the white eye of the moon, I returned home very slowly, remembering the words of my old pastor.

As I continued to meditate, I sensed a growing uneasiness. There wasn't any doubt about it . . . lately my day planner had replaced my Bible, condemning it, Monday through Friday, to an intolerable abandonment. I stopped for a moment to make the firm decision to begin to read it again and get back to loving it.

That night, as Mary rested, I sat on my balcony at home and looked out at the horizon. I held my Bible in my hands, and my fingers thumbed through the sacred pages, stroking them with gentleness.

This book had spoken to me so many times, and it had revealed so many beautiful truths to me.

I closed my eyes and prayed; then I opened them and began to read.

The letters transformed into beautiful gems. I held in my hands a treasure chest that had been forgotten, but now had been rescued. And I was determined to delight myself with the thousand gems that it contained.

My Bible, my beloved Bible . . . a treasure of invaluable worth.

An Unexpected Meeting

Summoned with Urgency

Great men and women are rarely isolated mountain-peaks;
they are the summits of huge ranges.

—THOMAS WENTWORTH

It was Friday.

The piercing sound of the telephone made me jump and suddenly drop the pen I was using to finish my sermon for the upcoming Sunday.

I looked at my watch. It was just a little before seven in the morning. The few calls that I had received at untimely hours had never been good.

My jolt turned to worry when I saw that the incoming number was from my old pastor.

I answered immediately.

"I'm sorry to bother you." Rachel's voice had an apologetic tone. "But my husband insists on seeing you as soon as possible."

151

"I will be right there, but tell me, is everything okay? Has something happened to your husband?"

"Not much, except his strength is failing even more, and he hasn't stopped insisting to me that he needs to talk with you."

Twenty minutes later, I was standing in front of the familiar blue door studded with black nails. I didn't even have time to grab the doorknob to announce my arrival. The door opened as if Rachel had been looking down from the window waiting impatiently for me to arrive.

"He's in his room," she told me.

The shadows under her eyes told me that she had spent the night with no sleep.

"Hello, son!"

The old man did not address me any other way now, and he stretched out his arms, welcoming me.

"Please forgive my whim of making you come when it's not Monday, and at this time of day, but there's something here"—he tapped his ribs two times lightly near his heart—"that is struggling to come out and I fear that Monday—"

I did not allow him to finish his sentence. Instead, I leaned over his bed and hugged him.

As always, he smelled of fresh cologne and soap. Rachel painstakingly groomed him to the point that his body exuded a clean aroma. His eyes, always moist because of his age, were also open windows to his immaculate inner being.

"I'm happy to see you," I told him. "I'm also having a hard time waiting until next Monday."

He wanted to go straight to the point. "I know that you already know the details of the sickness that plagues me."

In an extremely calm manner, he kept his gaze on my eyes and continued, "Cancer is one of the few evils they still cannot cure with modern drugs—"

"You mustn't lose hope," I interrupted him, "nor your faith."

"I keep both of them intact," he assured me. "Please forgive me if I sound arrogant, but I haven't lost one or the other. Nevertheless, I won't be the one who twists God's arm to dish out a miracle. He is wise and I am not. He knows what's best for me, and I don't know that. Therefore, I prefer to rest in His wisdom and calmly accept His wise plan." He sat up with difficulty to add emphasis to his message.

"But I didn't ask you to come here to speak about sicknesses. On that point, it's a waste of time to talk about details, as it is to recognize that I was a little stubborn in refusing to go to the doctor when the symptoms first started. Nonetheless, science is at a disadvantage against cancer. Surgery can remove it, as long as it hasn't spread too much; but in my case, I not only ignored it too long but it had the nerve to attack my pancreas, which eliminated the possibility of operating on it as well as surviving it. Unless God intervenes, and as I already told you, I don't discount it or demand it, but in a little while . . . a few days, or perhaps a few weeks, I will be dead."

A shudder plowed through my body, running from the bottom of my feet to the top of my head. My old pastor's transparency as well as his amazing fortitude left me speechless.

"Today I can talk about it with complete calmness, but don't believe it always was that way. When the doctors informed me of the unpleasant tenant that had lodged itself inside me, I almost keeled over. There I was, with only the hope of living for two to six months, getting more depressed by the hour, until He appeared."

"He?"

"God intervened," he clarified, "and He did it in a powerful way. My bed of sickness stopped being a torture rack and turned into an altar of worship. He turned the dark corridor that was leading to death into a delightful road that was drawing me near to life . . . to abundant life."

He smiled and leaned back, letting his body rest.

"But I didn't call you here to torment you with my woes," he said, looking at me and smiling. "As I told you, there is something weighing on my heart. A few days ago, I told you it was necessary for you to develop disciples, do you remember?"

I nodded my head in agreement, and then I recited like a diligent student: "There are five types of people: people with problems, good people, fellow warriors, *disciples*"—I emphasized this word, since he had just mentioned it—"and people with resources."

"Perfect score."

He smiled briefly, and then he took on a serious tone: "I really want to stress that aspect, that one about disciples. That one is essential if you want to serve God with joy and in a way that lasts. Do you realize that Jesus dedicated more of His time to a group of twelve instead of the masses?"

"That's right. It's something you get from reading the Gospels."

"Jesus made it a priority to form a team. He did it fast, at the beginning of His ministry, and He did it purposefully, dedicating a lot of prayer to His selection process, and with great zeal and investment of His time to the aspect of His training. Why do you think He made that issue so important?"

I intended to respond. I tried, but he didn't give me time. There was such urgency in his desire to speak that it affected his normal politeness and ability to listen.

"He wanted His ministry to go on after His death. He knew that these twelve men would continue to be His feet, hands, and mouth when He no longer was around."

He made a new attempt to sit up in the bed, but he didn't have the strength. I helped him and placed several pillows behind his back so that he could remain sitting up. Then he pointed out to me the small table that was in the far end of the room.

"Could you bring me that journal and fountain pen, please?"

On the first white page of paper he wrote three capital Ms, underlining them on purpose. He looked at me and asked: "Have you ever heard speak of the process of the three Ms?"

"Never," I admitted.

"It relates to an acrostic formed by three words."

He returned to his journal and completed the words:

+ Man
+ Movement
+ Monument

Once again he looked at me intently as he pointed at each of the words with his fountain pen.

"Listen, son."

His voice was still laced with urgency, the same with which he had summoned me to come this morning.

"God will take a man."

He underlined the word *Man*.

156

"He will use him powerfully, demonstrating His grace through him. That will cause a movement to begin."

He drew a circle around the second word. *Movement*.

"That movement will affect people who are involved in the mission, caught up with the project, and infected by the influence of that leader. No one is capable of measuring the powerful effect that a group of people touched by the hand of God and wisely led by a humble and consecrated servant can have."

There was a note of triumph in his voice, but his voice lowered in tone as he marked the next word with his fountain pen: *Monument*.

"Too frequently," he said, then repeated sadly, "I mean, quite often when a consecrated and charismatic leader dies, the movement that rose up under his influence and affected so many people begins to lose its fire until it finally dies out. The only thing that is left is a monument: 'in memory of.' A memory, cold as stone, of something that has died, but does not continue on. A divine presence that was, but is no longer here."

My eyes were fixed on the sheet of paper, reading the words over and over, and assimilating the powerful message they contained.

Then he cleared his throat for such a long time I thought that he was in agony, but he was only clearing his voice.

I almost jumped when I felt his cold hand on my forearm.

"Listen." He was talking quickly, as if he had a premonition that his time was running out or that he feared that he wouldn't be able to communicate this important truth to me.

"The only way to make sure that the fire doesn't go out when the torch gets extinguished is to make sure that it has lit up many more. Do you understand? Transfer the faith to others, infect many others with the fire, infect all those around us with the blessed virus of vision and passion. Form a team. That's what it's about, forming a team and inoculating each one of them with the passion that consumes us. Whoever makes this wise move will perpetuate the fire and will succeed in getting their church to continue affecting people, reaching the nations, and emptying out hell, even when the leader is no longer there. Don't work alone."

The pressure of his hand on my forearm and the fervor with which he spoke surprised me. "Tell me, son, do you understand what I'm saying to you?"

"Perfectly," I answered as I covered his hand with my other hand and nodded my head firmly in agreement with the message I had received.

"Servants who reproduce themselves in other servants. Paul in Timothy; Moses in Joshua; Elijah in Elisha."

He stopped for a moment, then right away continued with his talk: "In turn, Timothy, Joshua, and Elisha continued to multiply themselves. I must warn you that you will invest time in people who will fail you. But that possibility shouldn't discourage you. When you find someone who genuinely loves God and wants to serve Him, adopt him as a spiritual son and open up the treasure chest of your wisdom so that he assimilates it. It is the only way that the world will continue to be filled with living stones and not dead monuments . . . It is the way that this generation, and those to follow, will continue to have churches that are on fire and not religious cemeteries."

He almost had an edge of anger in his voice as he continued

to speak: "What does it matter that hundreds of pilgrims gaze at the stairs that Spurgeon climbed to stand behind his pulpit, if there is no voice behind that same pulpit that challenges human beings today? What benefit is it to visit the corner where Wesley kneeled so frequently that it wore down the wood, if altars are still not being built where knees bend down imploring a visitation from God? We do not want cold monuments, but rather torches that radiate light and warmth to a world that desperately needs them. And this will only happen by transferring a vibrant faith, a clear vision, and a passion that consumes us—"

"You've done that with me," I interrupted him, "and I'm grateful to you for it. Yet I never thought that I would be the one to take your place. Did you ever think that in picking me you had bet on a losing horse?"

Through the moisture of his eyes a smile beamed.

"I never thought that," he told me without wavering. "There is something more important than aptitude, the ability to do things, and that is attitude, the motivation and spirit with which things are done. Lou Holtz said it this way: 'Aptitude is what you are able to do. Motivation determines what you will do. Attitude determines how well you will do it.'"

He cleared his throat again and took a sip of water. His prescriptions dried his mouth out, but it still had wise sentences to declare; and for that reason, he went on again immediately. "I quickly saw in you more than an interest to 'do things right'; I saw you were interested in 'doing right things.' Do you understand the difference?"

I nodded in agreement again as I made the firm decision to

write down these phrases as soon as possible and meditate on them: "Attitude is more important than aptitude." "Doing things right is not the same as doing the right things."

My old pastor must have read my thoughts, because he enriched the reflection by adding, "An efficient servant is the one who knows how to do things right. An effective servant is the one who knows how to do the right things."

He waited the appropriate amount of time for me to assimilate the wisdom of the phrase, then he went on. "There are values more important than ability or talents, although these undoubtedly have their place of importance."

He took his Bible and looked through its pages. Even in this gesture, I could tell that his strength was leaving him; his fingers seemed lazy, as if the thin sheets of paper seemed like heavy rocks to him.

Finally, he found the text and turned the Bible toward me, pointing with his long finger at the part he wanted me to read: "And the things that you have heard from me among many witnesses, commit these to faithful men who will be able to teach others also" (2 Timothy 2:2).

I looked at him after reading it, and he unwrapped the hidden meaning in those words: "Do you see how Paul commissions his disciple to carry out the mission by delegating?"

"You're right," I admitted. "That's what you see from these verses."

"But that work must be entrusted to people who demonstrate two qualities: faithfulness and suitability. Can you appreciate the order in which those characteristics are related?"

"Yes. First faithful, and then suitable."

My confident answer caused a weak smile to form on his lips.

He made his next comment with words filled with conviction that left no doubt about his strongest held beliefs.

"I'm sure that it was a premeditated and carefully calculated order: first faithfulness, and then suitability. Faithfulness points to a character quality, and suitability to a set of abilities. This second one is important, but the first one is vital . . . absolutely essential. There are people capable of singing like angels or speaking with amazing eloquence, or gifted with tremendous organizational skills, or are influential leaders, but if they do not complement their suitability with the necessary faithfulness, not one of them will be capable of serving in the kingdom of God, because in that kingdom other values are prized, such as loyalty, humility, and faithfulness."

He looked at me and I nodded, letting him know that I understood him. Then he said to me, "Forgive me for bothering you again, but would you be so kind as to bring me that wooden doll in the third drawer?"

"Do you mean this?" I asked, surprised, showing him a Russian matryoshka, a nesting doll.

"Yes, that one."

He reached out his hand, and grabbing it, he held it in front of me.

"Do you know much about these dolls?"

"Well, not much. I believe that when they are opened they contain other smaller ones inside. I understand that inside one of them can be five or six that get smaller and smaller."

"You're right. Would you open them and put them in order on the table?"

I obeyed, though I didn't quite understand my old pastor's intentions.

I opened one after another, and from the inside of each one, I took out another, almost an exact twin except in size. Finally, I got to the last one, so small that it still couldn't have something inside, but this little wooden figure was wrapped in paper.

"Could you read what is written on that piece of paper?"

I read: "If we 'give birth' to servants smaller than us, we will become a church of dwarfs."

I looked at my old pastor; his eyes were riveted on mine. I read the phrase again.

The letters were as incredibly small as how incredibly large the truth they contained.

"Every doll is 'pregnant' with another one smaller in size," he said, and then went on to explain. "What is killing a lot of churches is the panic-that-they-will-leave-me-in-the-shadows syndrome. Leaders who show off their power accept the fact that other leaders will arise, yes, but 'not so they outshine me.' That fear causes them to hold back knowledge and strategies and not pour themselves into others or train them thoroughly. They fear being replaced. But congregations that are pastored by people determined to convert the church into a maternity ward that is constantly nurturing to capable servants that are gifted, trained, and humble . . . Those churches will be unstoppable. They will change the world and will have a powerful influence on society."

Before going on, he was quiet for a moment, as if he was catching his breath or trying to create the right moment.

"If God allows you to grow old in a church, don't grab hold of the pulpit and turn it into your power turf. Enjoy seeing new servants rise up. Churches that don't allow that transition end up dying when their pastor dies, and in many cases they are corpses for years, even though a death certificate hasn't been issued."

I looked at the wooden dolls, thinking about the obvious truth my old pastor had shared with me. I thought about the church I was pastoring and the promising young people and adults who were passionate about Jesus.

The voice of the venerable old man brought me back from my daydreaming.

"Arrange the dolls in the opposite order," he instructed.

I arranged them then not from largest to smallest, but the opposite way.

The old man pointed to the last one, which was now the largest.

"Would you like to read the text engraved on the base?"

I read: "If we give birth to servants who are more capable and gifted than we are, we will become a church of giants whose influence will be unstoppable."

"Create a team," he insisted. "The modern discovery of the laser light is nothing more than the concentration of light in a very fixed point, and that is something powerful. Your ministry will have authentic power if you succeed in concentrating *your* energy in your mission."

He emphasized the personal pronoun.

"Some servants empty their cartridges firing at many targets. Others concentrate their potential in one direction: their own. They invest their strength in that for which they were created and qualified for. *The secret of concentration lies in elimination.* If you're able to concentrate on your mission and eliminate other obligations from your agenda, you will leave indelible marks."

He was quiet for a moment on purpose so as to emphasize the next phrase: "Ask yourself if what you are doing today is moving you closer to where you want to be tomorrow."

Such sincere words were starting to make me feel uncomfortable, and I felt as though his talk were an X-ray of my daily activities.

I answered, and my voice held an edge of complaint. "But the church has many fronts. There are too many areas that require the pastor's presence."

"That's not true."

There was no anger in his voice but rather persistence. His smile softened his resounding objection somewhat.

"It's true that a church has a lot of areas that require attention, but saying that all of them have to be taken care of by the pastor is equivalent to assuming that a flock of sheep grows because the shepherd gives birth to the little lambs in the flock and then takes charge of nursing them, taking care of them, and taking them out to graze. It's sheep that give birth to new sheep. The shepherd should watch over the fold, but there are responsibilities, a lot of them, that should be taken care of by other people in the fold. The effectiveness of a pastor lies in his ability to concentrate his energies in the work he is responsible for."

He clearly insisted that the phrase be turned into a motto: "The secret of concentration lies in elimination."

"I agree."

My voice was still uneasy and held a hint of challenge in my question: "And the rest of the issues? What do I do with them?"

"Delegate them."

His patience was as admirable as his absolute certainty.

"And that can only be achieved by creating a team. Other people will be your eyes, hands, and feet in the different places where you cannot go. You need to be prepared, however, that some of your disciples will fail you. Including some of the most promising ones."

Again his smile softened the seriousness of the message he was conveying to me.

"Not even Jesus was free from that circumstance. Disciples have a varied effect on our life. At times God allows us to see the fruit of our investment as we see them turn into effective workers, but at other times they make us sad by their lack of commitment, their immature responses, or their carnal reactions. Don't give up when that happens, because for every servant who fails, God will put others by your side who are faithful and loyal."

Again silence settled down between us. A reflective silence, filled with feelings. I had a lot of questions, but it wasn't the time to ask them. It was time to meditate and assimilate the wisdom that filled every corner of his bedroom, and that continued to sink in my mind.

"Look, son," he said as he reached out his hand and took out a photograph from the drawer of the little table near the head-board. "Look at this picture."

The photo was of a strange flower with orange tones and an extraordinary size.

"The scientific name of this flower is *rafflesia arnoldii*." He made a face, almost as if saying, *What a name!*, but the ease with which he pronounced the unpronounceable name surprised me, as if he had familiarized himself with that strange flower on purpose to meditate about it. "It holds the record," he went on, "for being the largest flower that exists. It can reach ten feet in diameter and a hundred sixty-five pounds in weight; it grows at a speed of four inches per day."

He looked at me, amused at my expression of surprise. "But, curiously, they call it the 'corpse flower.' Do you know why?"

I didn't answer because I didn't have an answer, and I also knew that he wouldn't wait for me to give one.

"The reason that this rarity of nature has such a dismal name is because it holds another record not so honorable: it's the most foul-smelling flower that exists. It gives off a nauseating and rotten odor like a corpse that has been dead for a few days."

"Impressive," I replied.

My old pastor was apparently directing his talk toward an unforgettable conclusion, and he looked at me firmly: "When you go to select your intimate circle, be extremely careful. Jesus spent the night praying to God before recruiting His disciples. Use your knees more than your eyes in your mission to form a team. Prayer will clear your sight and will give you the sufficient depth so as not to be easily impressed with flamboyant talents. Don't be deceived by prodigious growth, and always doubt the magical formulas of the newcomers. Don't listen to the con artists that come to you with their chests full of medals. I like stable trajectories better than meteoric blastoffs. I've already seen too many fireworks, too many flowers that are flashy from a distance but are toxic when you're near them, giants from afar and cadavers up close. As I told you, pride stinks, and that stench will dull the shine of the noblest material."

I remained silent. I could sense my old pastor still had something to tell me.

"In contrast, there are incredibly valuable treasures that are extremely small in size. Did you know that in your middle ear there is a tiny bone that is the smallest in your whole body? It is only nine-hundredths of an inch long, and yet its function is vital. It's called the stirrup, and along with the anvil and the hammer, it captures the vibrations from the eardrum and amplifies sound waves. It allows us to hear."

He stopped for a moment, and his face took on the expression of daydreaming. With his gaze fixed on heaven, as if contemplating with delight that singular type of people that he was going to refer to, he said, "I've seen them so many times! I've thoroughly enjoyed thinking about them. Unassuming people, almost simple to a point! They pass by unnoticed, but they capture the divine whisper and bring it close to others. They are not huge flowers that demand their own showcases. No. They detest pedestals and prefer corners, and in doing so they are in tune with God, who searches for His best instruments among the humble. When God finds a humble instrument, what a magnificent rendition He performs through it. The notes that follow then really do bring heaven's pure air closer . . . authentic spiritual oxygen."

His speech had lost the sense of urgency, recapturing the calmness of the last days. He spoke slowly, as if the moment did not demand the least amount of hurriedness. Even his breathing had a more measured cadence, and an almost tangible peace could be seen in his eyes.

"I had so much I had to say to you, son. Once again I'm sorry for asking you to come, but now I feel much more at peace. What I had shared with you was weighing too heavy on me to wait until next Monday. Even after you've forgotten all the rest, remember this, please."

He grasped my right hand with his, as if he feared I would leave without listening to his crucial reflection: "When the time comes to choose your team, don't let yourself be dazzled by people's abilities. The essence of people is not found in their last names, nor in their expertise or talents. Look deeper inside. Character is more important than ability. You won't find perfect servants, but look for those who are aiming for perfection. Don't let yourself be impressed by the eloquence of their words or how amazing their credentials are. Look at the heart. A clean heart is worth more than a showcase full of trophies. Look at the heart," he repeated. "Do they love God? Are they seeking to live in holiness? Are they faithful to their spouses? Upright in their businesses? Do their words carry the weight of a contract? Do they show evidence of spiritual fruit? Hell will be full of eloquent speakers and singers who sing perfectly in tune. There will be no lack of influential leaders there . . . but what won't be in hell is one single Christian character."

He smiled as he patted my arm with affection.

"That's right, so spur them on toward excellence. God doesn't deserve mediocre servants who don't care about details. They must study conscientiously and prepare themselves seriously. They mustn't despise seminaries, institutes, or any educational center of proven consistency. Teach them to shoot for the moon, because whoever aims for the moon will end up hitting some star. God doesn't deserve irresponsible soldiers who only are willing to 'play church.' What He is looking for are committed people who take this seriously . . . so seriously that they put their lives into it. If they bring their *attitude*, God will take care of the *aptitude*. God will take care of training them."

As if caressing the room with his eyes, he looked around it until he ended up fixing his eyes on me. They were tired but glowed with pure determination. His look seemed to me to be one of apology.

"Forgive me for so much chatter. Rachel often tells me, 'Sweetheart, what would music be without the pauses? Words are silver, but silence is golden.' But as it would appear, I don't pay much attention to that. Forgive me for taking so much of your time. I can assure you, now I feel much more at peace."

"Then it's been worth it," I told him. "What I've learned today will stay with me my whole life."

We looked at each other. It was a long moment, almost endless. We scrutinized each other, I believe, to see if the transference of wisdom had happened.

My old pastor managed a slight smile.

"Good-bye, my son."

I leaned over his bed to say good-bye, and it seemed strange how long his hug lasted. When I straightened up the old man was crying. He kept my right hand between his while he gazed at me from behind a curtain of tears. He moved his lips but no words came out. Finally, he said a short and gentle, "Good-bye."

To me it was a heartrending good-bye.

He did not say, "See you next Monday," nor, "Until the next time," but, "Good-bye."

And in his tears, I couldn't help seeing a letter written in the form of a good-bye. I felt as if his crying would drown me.

I left his room as fast as I could, because the knot in my throat was suffocating me, and I did not want to cry in front of him.

It was out in the street, in front of the rosebush, where I gave free rein to my emotions, and the image of the new red rose that was beginning to open ended up being drenched by the watery curtain of my tears.

As I looked through the tears in my eyes, it seemed to me as if the group of roses that had formed a perfect cross was beginning to wilt.

The Last Monday

The Dream

They may cut down all the flowers, but they will not be able to stop spring from coming.

—Pablo Neruda

It was Monday.

I didn't sleep well, and I woke up very early.

I had been up for a long time when I opened up the windowed balcony and saw how the dawn was slowly rising over the city. The orange on the horizon was slowly growing larger. The far north was beginning to also turn green with unrelenting exquisiteness.

I've seen the sunrise hundreds of times, but yet today . . . why did I feel that it was so different?

It was Monday.

The day I would meet with my old pastor. But a growing uneasiness was weighing on my chest and choking my throat. Perhaps it was because of the short dream that I had—or rather had me—that woke me up with a start so that I couldn't get back to sleep last night.

In the dream I saw myself traveling through an arid and hot land—a desert. The top of the ground was cracked and so hot that it gave off puffs of smoke. I was walking fatigued, at the point of exhaustion; yet I was moving forward with determination, as if I knew my exact route and also my destination.

As I came to the top of a dune, I saw it suddenly . . .

"What did you see?"

The voice behind me startled me. When I turned around, I looked into Mary's eyes and her irresistible smile. My story, narrated out loud unconsciously, had woken her up.

"It woke me when I heard you speaking alone," she said, smiling. "What was it that you saw?"

"The cross. I was there, in the heart of the desert. It was lifted up . . . breathtaking and powerful. But what most caught my attention was that it was covered in green leaves and roses, as if spring had burst forth on the dry wood. The roses that covered it—all red—were unusually large, and their petals shone like glass."

"It was a lovely dream," Mary said to me, wrapping her arm around my waist. "I don't understand why you're so distressed."

"It's because I didn't see him!"

"Who didn't you see?"

"I was looking for my old pastor. I looked for him everywhere, shading my eyes with my hand and looking in every direction, but he wasn't there."

"Was he supposed to be there?"

"Yes, he was supposed to be there because he was there in my earlier dream, don't you remember? He was kneeling at the foot of the cross, signaling to me with one hand and pointing to the cross with the other. But now he's not there."

A tremulous silence hung between us, a muted moment filled with forebodings.

The lamp of memory lit up the motto of our old pastor in my mind, and I recited it: "I was born in the shade of the cross. I want to live anchored to it, and may it be the ladder that lifts me up to His presence when my time comes."

"It could be . . ."

Mary didn't finish her sentence, and in her eyes I could read the word *fear* written there.

"Perhaps . . ."

She didn't dare continue.

"Perhaps . . ." I finished the sentence that she was afraid to say, "he is not in the shade of the cross because it has already become his ladder."

Concern overwhelmed her then, and she said, "Tell me about the dream again. Tell me everything you saw."

The anxiety of her question did not help my peace. On the contrary, her nervousness made mine grow. I told her again all that I had dreamed.

"Wait!" I told her. "I remember something more. At the end of my dream, I was looking at the highest point of the cross, and from there I was looking at the clouds, a lot of clouds, infinite white clouds that seemed to indicate the only way to go was: higher, higher . . . until the far reaches of heaven!"

When I finished, I looked at my watch. It was five thirty

in the morning. Despite the untimely hour, I couldn't wait, so I started to get dressed.

Mary got dressed faster than me and was pulling on me even before I had buttoned my shirt.

"Let's go!"

She walked toward the door without letting go of me. The pressure of her hand on mine was hurting me. Nervously, she insisted again, "Let's go! We have to go see them!"

We stopped a few feet from the blue door.

Everything was silent . . . even more than usual.

The birds were quiet.

Even the wind had stopped, giving the surroundings an almost gloomy touch.

"What a shocking calmness," Mary said, not daring to raise her voice above a whisper.

I kept quiet, but I wanted to say that more than calmness, what we sensed was death.

A dizziness rose from my stomach, growing and gnawing. My heart felt sad, and a strong pressure in my throat made it hard to breathe; it was the foreboding of being left an orphan. I had to lean against a tree, because I was about to faint.

After a few moments in which I caught my breath, and was helped by Mary, we slowly crossed the last stretch and stopped two steps in front of the house just as the door opened and Rachel appeared.

Her eyes focused on ours with an infinite serenity, despite the fact that on her retina were imprinted a thousand messages of good-bye.

It wasn't even necessary for her to say it; her eyes had already shouted it: he was no longer there.

Rachel was not crying.

Not even when Mary ran toward her and hugged her, nor when I drew near and kissed her cheek, articulating an awkward, "I'm so sorry."

Not even when the three of us hugged one another for a long time, not knowing what to say.

We didn't know what to say, and she didn't need us to say anything.

After a few minutes that seemed like several lifetimes, Rachel pulled away and looked at us again with eyes, that today appeared more solemn rather than sad and desolate. They reminded me of two parts of the sea, in which the waters were turbulent and agitated.

"He is with Him."

Her words swayed back and forth like feathers before resting on our souls.

"He has slipped from life sweetly, without losing his peace or his calmness or his smile. He is with Him," she repeated, nodding her head slightly. "That was his last wish. Last night, before going to sleep, he turned toward me, and kissing me, he said, 'See you later.' It seemed strange to me, but I fell asleep thinking, *Of course, we will see each other in the morning.*"

She remained quiet to compose herself.

"But that wasn't what he wanted to tell me . . . It wasn't that, no. He already felt that God was calling him, and he was talking about that morning when good-byes will never again rip the soul."

As she was talking, I remembered the word that sealed our last meeting. "Good-bye," he had said while he was crying, and every one of his tears had conveyed the same message.

Rachel continued giving the details of what had happened that morning: "When I woke up and didn't see him, I got scared. I looked for him in the kitchen. As soon as he would get up, he would have his coffee. 'It recharges my batteries,' he would say. But there was no aroma of coffee in the house, but rather an emptiness. Did you know that absence leaves a peculiar smell? It is an indescribable smell . . . Nonetheless, I kept looking for him. I looked on the porch, where he often enjoyed watching the sunrise, and I felt that 'night' was coming when I didn't find him in his chair or see the little birds that would come to eat the breadcrumbs he would toss to them."

She was quiet for a moment and almost managed a smile.

"I finally found him, and I don't know why I didn't think of it! He was in his office, knelt down on his old cushion. It was his greatest delight, his inescapable necessity. That did not just recharge his batteries . . . That gave him life."

Rachel continued her story, caught up in it, as if reliving the moment as she shared it with us: "Even from the door I knew that only a rough shell of a body rested on that cushion. He was already flying through a much higher heaven . . . he was already breathing air that is much purer."

I felt a strange trembling. I didn't ever remember being overwhelmed by such an intense emotion.

Mary was not speaking. She was looking at the ground, where the moisture from her tears had formed a tiny pool.

I returned toward the house . . . toward the open door. With all my strength I wanted to see my old pastor appear with his outstretched arms, as always, extending his loving welcome to me.

Turning my face to Rachel, with a look I asked her permission to go see him, and she granted it. Only then did I enter and look for his office . . . that little room that for so many Mondays had been a haven of confidences and a healing room for my soul.

I saw his cushion.

There he was . . . I took the same seat I had every day, in front of him, and I looked at him. Oh, how much wisdom had sprung forth from that worn-out cushion!

That chair had held so much authority! And what an enormous emptiness it held now!

Trapped by an unbearable attack of loneliness, I looked down, and my eyes rested on the cushion that was lying on the floor.

It still held the marks from my old pastor.

I drew near and rested my knees on the indents that his had made. I could have sworn that the cloth was hot, as if a living torch had lit it and now that same flame was catching me on fire.

"At times I kneel down undone, but I always get up remade." Those had been his words.

And as I worshipped, I discovered the essence of that message.

It could have been a few minutes or several hours before I felt Mary kneel down at my side. We shared the cushion, and I had the beautiful sensation that together on our knees our souls were united as well.

She looked at me as she whispered, "Someone needs to fill this place . . . Someone needs to continue his work."

I took her hand as we closed our eyes in prayer.

"Here I am, Lord . . ."

The words sprung from my lips at the same time tears filled my eyes.

"Here I am, here I am . . ."

"Here we are . . ."

Mary's voice echoed mine.

"Here we are, Lord . . ."

When Rachel came near and lightly rested her hands on our heads, we felt as if a new time in our lives was being inaugurated. We were being commissioned.

Through my tear-filled eyes, I saw our united hands, and beneath them, like fire, glowed the stitched cross that decorated the cushion.

I knew that I had finally found my place . . . our place. Sheltered beneath the cross . . . kneeling on top of it.

It was late afternoon when we left the house. I still seemed like morning to me, but yet the sun, little by little, had surrendered, and the night began imposing its kingdom of shadows. But not inside me, because a new day had begun there.

That's when I saw it. The ground, next to the door, seemed carpeted in red petals.

The roses had shed their petals.

Some scraggly petals were still hanging on and swaying in the breeze, but the majority of them had scattered over the ground. Those flowers that had bloomed in rhythm with his wise counsels had said goodbye with him. Now they were only dark brown stains crowning a stalk.

I remembered the dream from that night: the red roses covered the cross. My old pastor was no longer there, but the flowers that had bloomed in the warm breath of his counsels completely covered the ground.

I bent down next to the tub and one by one picked up those petals that seemed like letters full of wisdom.

After straightening them out carefully, I put them in my pocket.

We kissed Rachel, who wouldn't let us stay with her that night.

"Thank you," she told us. "Others wanted to come and be with me, but I told them all that I wanted to be alone with him these last moments."

"That's fine, Rachel," Mary said to her as she hugged her good-bye. "We'll see you tomorrow."

"Wait!" she said when we had hardly gone fifty feet.

She entered the house and returned almost immediately.

"Take it," she told me, handing me a small wooden chest, decorated with designs made out of something similar to mother-of-pearl. One that stood out was a large cross. "The contents kept him busy these last days and some of his nights. He worked diligently, knowing that his time was running out. I'm sure that it is important. He asked me to give it to you when he . . . when he no longer was here. When I saw him this morning, knelt down, he still had his fountain pen in his hand, and the tip of it was still dripping ink over the last word he had written. It is for you. He told me to give it to you."

I took the gift as if it were the greatest treasure in the world.

"We will see you tomorrow," we promised as we hugged her again.

A little while later, Mary and I, as well as nightfall, all arrived home at the same time.

Then I realized that we had spent Rachel's first day as a widow together, and we hadn't eaten anything. Yet neither of us felt hungry.

We arrived early at the wake.

✢

"Come in."

Rachel took my and Mary's hand and gently pulled us along. She led us next to my old pastor's body.

I drew near to pay my respects. It seemed impossible that this face so full of peace belonged to a dead man.

His facial expression was serene. His white hair was brushed back and seemed to radiate a profound peace. His eyes looked as if he was asleep, and his mouth, slightly open, showed his teeth in a peaceful smile.

As I looked at him intently, it seemed as if he was breathing. I felt as if at any moment he would open his eyes and say to me: "Let me tell you a story."

Over his body rested his Bible with a gold-embossed cross that shone. That image was very familiar to me. It was the one I saw those last Mondays, except now the book was closed. From the headboard, a large metal cross projected its shadow over him, as if it were protecting him. An empty cross, as he always used to say, "He endured the cross for us, but the cross did not hold Him back. He became man so He could die. But He continues being God so He can save."

As I watched him, it seemed as if at any moment he would open his mouth and declare his deepest wish: "I was born in the shadow of the cross, I want to live anchored to it, and may it be the ladder that lifts me up into His presence when my time comes."

"You have attained it now, my old pastor," I whispered to him. "You have fulfilled your dream." And then close to his ear, I added, "And it wasn't anything stupid what you said to Joseph . . . your son. Now you've proven it, haven't you? It wasn't absurd when you said, 'We'll see each other soon.'"

"Take it," Rachel said to me, pointing to the Bible that was resting on the chest of her husband.

"But . . . but," I stuttered, not daring to reach out my hand.

"It's for you," she insisted. "He told me, 'When my time comes, I want him to have this book, so that he continues loving it and proclaiming it.' That's what he told me."

I felt excited, and I felt scared. Both feelings were fighting with each other to see which one would win.

I finally stretched out my hand, which was visibly trembling, and rested it first on top of my old pastor's chest. I could swear that I felt warmth, as if beneath that dark suit a flame of passion was still lit, or as if that sacred book continued sending fire to the core of his being.

My fingers tightened around the Bible. Yet my hand was still shaking so much that Mary stretched out hers and held the Bible with me. Her fingers seemed white as they tightened near mine . . . and between our hands shone the printed cross.

"Here we are, Lord," she said.

And as I looked at her, I saw a large tear fall from her closed eyes and then slide down her cheek.

We were determined to accompany Rachel to her home, even though she insisted she could go by herself.

It was a delightful time that we had talking together; in fact, we laughed as we remembered some of my old pastor's stories. And as I heard Rachel's crystal-clear laughter, I thought of how wonderful it was to know that we cannot feel like a total orphan when God is with us.

The words of Khalil Gibran echoed in my mind: "No matter how long the storm lasts, the sun always shines again in the clouds."

"We will see each other a lot," Mary promised.

"You don't have to do it for me," Rachel replied.

"We're not doing it for you," I explained. "We're doing it for us."

As we said good-bye, the night was beginning to fall, but the dying sun still cast sharp beams of light over the quiet countryside, giving me the impression that it was lighting up a new road for us.

When we arrived home, we were struck with all the emotions from that intense day. The blood drained from our heads, and we collapsed on our bed.

"Just five minutes of sleep before I open the chest and look at its contents," I told myself, "just five minutes."

But my eyes closed and I slept for hours.

I opened my eyes much later, midway through a gray and rainy morning. It was about noon on a day in the middle of November.

Mary was resting at my side, as well as the reality that he

was no longer here, which overwhelmed me as soon as I finally became conscious.

It was Sunday morning, and I had woken up early.

I never used to dream, but now I hardly did anything else, and in my dream I saw myself in the desert as usual. The same sand dunes, the same avenging sun that made the ground burn, lifting wisps of smoke above it.

And the same cross . . .

But there was something more—something different.

This time it was me in the dream, and with frantic movements and anguished shouts, I was calling out to people who were plowing through that burning hell without noticing the cross. At the end of their strength, too many of them were dragging themselves along, unable to see the shade and life that were offered at the foot of the cross.

I woke up startled, waving my arms and with my forehead covered in sweat. The sheets seemed to be on fire, as if I had brought the fire of that desert back to my bed.

Fortunately, Mary continued to sleep. I didn't want to worry her with my frequent nights without sleep, though I couldn't get out of my mind the idea that together we had crossed a line that now placed us in a new time and a new dimension in our service to God.

I knew we would have to talk about it.

As I wiped away the sweat with the back of my hand, I sensed a growing uneasiness. It was like facing an unknown route without out a map. I sat up slowly, trying not to wake Mary, and I slipped my feet into my slippers to head for the kitchen. The first cup of coffee usually works wonders, especially when I wake up bothered by some dream, as I did this morning. As I was about to head for the door, my eyes noticed the wooden chest that rested on the little table. I had left it there the day Rachel had given it to me, but the rush with which things had happened had caused me to forget about it.

It was early, and there was still plenty of time to open the small church, so I took the chest, prepared a coffeepot, and was ready to uncover the chest's secret as I sipped the steaming coffee that would help wake me up.

I tried to undo the latch that closed the chest, but I got so nervous trying to do it that I made the iron prong and latch jump.

On the inside were piled various tiny, rolled-up parchments with a red ribbon that tightly held a dry red rose to each of them. As I looked more carefully, I discovered there were sixteen parchments, and they were all numbered.

With a trembling hand, I untied the ribbon from the first one. I removed the rose very carefully and unrolled the parchment.

At the head of the parchment was painted a cross, and the handwriting began right below it. By the weak and wavy strokes, I knew right away it was my old pastor's handwriting. The ink that had been used showed that it had been written with the same fountain pen.

"It seems like a posthumous legacy," I whispered, surprised, after reading the first words. And it was.

It was a posthumous legacy that would become now and forever the map that I needed for this new path.

Yet in that moment, I still did not realize it, nor could I even suspect it.

We had arrived at the church early. The short trip only takes us about ten minutes, but that day we rode in silence.

Mary was meditating, and so was I. I was thinking about the advice and wisdom of all that I had read that morning.

I was holding the worn, large-print Bible in one hand, and in the other I held the wooden chest that contained the parchments—both gifts from my old pastor.

I entered the church, which was filled with the dark cold of November, and Mary took her place near the door. From there she can watch over the church members after greeting them. She intercedes for people she notices who are sad, gives praise for those who are happy, and prays for those who are absent. From there she prays for me as well.

The short musical introduction that day was inspiring, and I could breathe in the sacred quietness in the air as I took my place behind the pulpit.

I opened my Bible and looked at it for a few seconds. Then I looked one by one at those who were seated, waiting for the sermon.

I looked at them and felt the love I had for them.

They were looking at me, and I knew that they loved me.

Way in the back, near the door, there he was: the man who had destroyed us with poisoned darts on the telephone. Nevertheless, today I stared at him and smiled . . .

He lowered his head, and I didn't feel any resentment. On the contrary, I felt filled with the "oxygen" of sincere affection.

Mary was close by me. She responded to my look with a smile, and then she nodded her head. I know she does that to pray for me. I know she loves me . . . I know that I love her. I need her so much.

Just when I was about to start my message, the door to the church opened, and Rachel entered.

Her white hair, carefully gathered up, was a faithful reflection of the purity of her soul. Her eyes still looked like two pieces from the sea with turbulent waters, but her smile was like the sun coming out, triumphant, above an ocean of clouds.

She sat down next to my wife and took hold of her hand.

Then she looked at me.

The light that shone from her face reached me, and I began to speak.

I tried to preach the sermon that I had prepared . . . the same one I was working on that Friday when I was called urgently to the house of my old pastor.

I tried to preach it, but I couldn't.

Only a few words sprang to my lips: "My life has sprung forth from the shade of the cross. I have always lived in the shadow of it, and I want the cross to be the ladder that lifts me up to His presence when my time comes."

I walked up then to the simple cross that was in the front of the altar and knelt in front of it. I stayed there, perhaps for about one minute, when I noticed that someone was kneeling together with me and had grabbed my hand. When I felt a ring press into my palm, I had the same feeling from when we would walk together with our fingers linked together . . . it was Mary.

I raised my head and saw Rachel's head bowed down. She too was kneeling close to the cross.

And then more and more people spontaneously came up to fill the floor around the altar.

Even he—the one who had called us on the telephone—had bowed his head, and I heard him crying . . . He came a little closer and took my free hand, the left one. When I looked at him, his trembling lips were saying two words, as short as they were powerful: "I'm sorry."

I stood up, and he did too; then we melted into a hug of reconciliation. I had the impression that the tears that were streaking down his face were the ice that had covered his heart. The heat of forgiveness had melted it.

I looked then and discovered that the benches of the church were empty . . . as empty as the altar was full.

Everyone was there, kneeling in the shadow of the cross.

I understood then that Mary and I weren't the only ones who had begun a new time in our lives. The church had embarked on a new phase.

When the emotional service had ended, we accompanied Rachel to her home. We didn't talk about much along the way, but still the moments of silence at her side seemed filled with peace.

Beside the blue door studded with black nails we said goodbye to one another.

Her smile projected the serenity of her soul. She hugged us as she said, "Thank you for continuing on with the work. The world needs people who have made the decision to love to the point of surrendering their lives to this endeavor."

We continued to hug one another for a few seconds, and during that time my eyes focused on the rosebush where every Monday night I would stop.

Something caught my attention . . . something extraordinary and powerful that made me pull away from the hug and walk over to the large tub.

I rubbed my eyes and looked again.

"How is that possible?"

I pointed at the rosebushes with insistence . . . because no words came out.

Fifteen red roses were blooming among the white flowers that were gleaming in the late afternoon sun . . . Fifteen new roses that were full of life.

"How is that possible?" I whispered again.

I ran toward the wooden chest that I had left moments ago on top of the circular stone bench covered with flowerpots.

The parchments were still in their place, carefully rolled up and tied with red ribbon. But the dry roses that were fastened to each one of them had disappeared.

The wilted ones had disappeared, and new flowers had bloomed.

"How is it possible that they have come back to life?" I repeated. "How can it be? Have I misplaced the dry flowers and these have appeared by coincidence?"

Rachel did not seem surprised. "I don't believe in coincidence."

She looked at us peacefully and explained, "Luck doesn't exist. God doesn't play dice. What may seem casual or extraordinary to us may be a message that God is shouting at us with a megaphone." She pointed at the rosebush as she continued to explain in a voice as peaceful as soothing. "These flowers bloomed from the warmth of eternal advice . . . from immutable principles that will keep the flame of service to God alive . . . They are values that never will die. That is why these flowers go on living."

We returned home very slowly.

Everything was quiet.

Off in the distance a dog let out a bark, reminding us that life went on, but not as quiet and beautiful as this.

My left hand squeezed the Bible that Rachel had given me. "It's for you," she had told me. "He asked me to give it to you. 'When my time comes, I want him to take this book, and continue to love and proclaim it.'"

Though it was an immense privilege, at the same time I felt a great weight of responsibility from which a thousand questions arose: *Will I be able to continue the work worthily? Will I be ready to do it? Will I have sufficient strength?*

Then I felt the pressure of Mary's fingers in my hand. I looked at her, and she smiled at me.

I am not alone in this mission; we are a team.

We stopped for a moment to look at the house again.

The chimney that rose up a number of feet cast a shadow, which along with the outline of the rooftop formed the same image of a cross, and I noticed that we were standing exactly on top of it.

Our feet were firmly planted on top of the same cross that endowed the ministry of our old pastor with power and glory . . .

We are not alone in this mission. Not everything depends upon us . . . almost nothing depends on us . . . we are a team headed up by the One who knows no defeat.

We started walking again.

We moved forward slowly, step-by-step over the long mast of that perfect cross that has forever turned into our path.

"So can I finally look inside of that mysterious chest?" Mary asked me when we arrived home.

"I looked inside this morning, and it has changed my life," I answered her.

"Well, what are we waiting for? It's time for it to change mine too."

We sat on the sofa, and as she held the small chest, I pulled out the parchment that was marked number one.

When you read this I will no longer be here. I mean, I will not be at your side, although the reality is that I will be there in the fullest sense of the word: I will have finished my race, and I will be enjoying the long-awaited reward of gazing at my Lord face-to-face. Thank you for your faithful company on the last stretch of my journey. Thank you for accepting the challenge of carrying on the work and beginning to plow the ground that others of us have dedicated our entire lives to.

I have decided to sum up in the way of a memorandum the principles that we have shared together Monday to Monday. Remembering them will be useful to you.

If I helped anyone, if what I did served for anything, I owe it to the grace of God and the determination with which I kept these principles. Henry Van Dyke aptly said, "What you possess in the world will be found at the day of your death to belong to someone else. But what you are will be yours forever." I take with me the best: my salvation, the knowledge of having lived to fulfill my highest purpose, and the joy of having done it beside the person whom I loved with all my heart: Rachel. The little that I leave, I want you to preserve my most precious legacy: this bouquet of flowers in the form of principles that will give life and authority to your ministry. I have named them: fifteen red roses, like drops that fall from the cross. Red, like the blood that stained the cross and upon which all that we are and do is sustained. Roses, like the ones that surprised you every Monday, opening up in the middle of the night. And roses, too, to remind you that the most sought-after flower can harbor sharp thorns, and whoever wants to show the world their beauty will have to do it at the risk of marking their path with blood.

Ministry is no different. Often we exercise it in the radiant sunshine of midday, but there are fruits that only mature under the light of the moon, and plants of tremendous beauty that grow in dark places. That is why at times it gets dark.

I suggest you memorize and live by these principles. Do not underestimate them for having emerged from the shaky hand of this old pastor. Remember that sometimes a broken watch is able to tell the exact time.

One last and meaningful request: take care of Rachel. She is the greatest treasure that God has given me on this earth.

Let me now finish. I will first list the principles and then in detail examine them one by one: When you want, you can begin to unravel the meanings of this bouquet of roses.

Principle Number One

Everything begins with loving God. Either we love the One we serve, or our service will become arduous and boring work. Don't work for the church of God; serve the God of the church.

Principle Number Two

Watch over and preserve the health of your family. One of the most powerful credentials of your ministry is your family, beginning with your marriage.

Principle Number Three

Spend quality time with your Bible. Any other book informs; the Bible transforms. All the others contain facts; the Bible contains power.

Principle Number Four

You either love those you serve, or you will stop serving them. It is impossible to dedicate your life to serving those you do not love. When love runs out, the joy of serving turns into obligation and hope into disappointment.

Principle Number Five

You are valuable. You are not one in a million, but rather one in six billion people who inhabit this earth. Only you can be you.

Principle Number Six

Be willing to forgive. It is impossible to move forward under the weight of resentment. And at the same time, be willing to forgive yourself. When you make a mistake, remember that a failure is not failing; failure is not trying again.

Principle Number Seven

Always stay grounded and levelheaded. After your greatest triumphs remember that your feet are still made of clay. Get over your failures, but don't allow your triumphs to defeat you.

Principle Number Eight

Pray. Make prayer a habit. Minutes spent with God make the day profitable. Hours spent with Him make life triumphant.

Principle Number Nine

Laugh as much as you can, and do it daily. Laughing has healing properties, and it is a gift from heaven. Walk, run, play, and laugh.

Principle Number Ten

Greatness is knowing how to be humble. God is not looking for shining stars; He prefers vessels of clay to minister His treasure.

Principle Number Eleven

Respond faithfully to the One who has chosen you. Faithfulness is demonstrated by staying where God has placed us, even though our parcel of land is located on the toughest slope of the mountain.

Principle Number Twelve

Learn the tremendous value of trials and difficulties. The most beautiful skies are always related to the darkest places, and the most difficult times are doors to better opportunities.

Principle Number Thirteen

Changes in the night? Never! Wait for morning to come. Don't make changes during times of storm. (Augustine of Hippo)

Principle Number Fourteen

Honesty: a highly prized value in heaven and earth. Who and what you are come before what you do. Your life comes before your job.

Principle Number Fifteen

Learn to form a team. Jesus discipled a few to send them out to many. The key to effectiveness is not in doing the work but in recognizing who the right person is to do it.

Inside the chest were fifteen parchments. Each of them explained and analyzed one of the principles.

With growing curiosity, Maria took the second parchment and handed it to me opened. It was then that I noticed my old pastor's fountain pen on top of it.

It was the same one that he had used his whole life; the one he wrote his powerful sermons with, and the one he used to write this impressive memorandum.

He had wanted to give it to me, and I knew that this gesture meant handing over his baton in this relay race. There were still lines to write, and now the pen was in my hand.

"Let's read the parchments!" Mary said to me, full of emotion.

Together we read the first one, and then another, and another . . . until we had emptied the large chest. It was my second time of reading them, but I still was moved by the immense volume of wisdom.

Next to the last word was a smear: like a tear of ink that the fountain pen had spilled, as if sensing the final heartbeat of my old pastor.

With the parchments still outspread, I knelt down, and Mary knelt at my side. I took the fountain pen, and beneath the smear of ink, with a hand that trembled as much as the one that had written this powerful memorandum, I wrote:

I purpose to be a faithful successor of my old pastor.

I purpose to put into practice every one of these principles.

I purpose to accept with dignity the blows that come and lift the cross up high.

When we picked up the parchments and put them back into the wooden chest, Mary noticed something.

"Look!" she said to me, lifting out a small paper that had remained in the bottom of the chest. "There's something written on it."

She read it aloud:

When life turns hard, and darkness hovers around you; when the
slope seems too steep and the weight becomes too much, return to
these principles. The last ones are crucial, but the first ones are too . . .

"That's strange!" Mary replied. "Doesn't his insistence seem
excessive?"

There was something strange about that sentence, but I
didn't have the strength to figure it out now. I had had enough
feelings for one day. The best thing we could do was rest. We
would see everything clearer tomorrow.

We slept deeply. The vortex of emotions had left us exhausted,
but sleep proved to be very healing. At six o'clock in the morning,
I opened my eyes and suddenly felt the fearful shudder that was
so familiar.

It was a mixture of hope for the future and fear for what was
to come—expectation about the new stage of life and fear of being
left an orphan, which the death of my old pastor represented.

With my arms under my head, I lay sprawled in bed looking
up at the ceiling . . . at the darkness that covered the ceiling.

Not even three minutes had gone by when Mary woke up.
She opened her eyes and sat up startled.

"The principles!" she shouted, startling me.

"What's the matter with you?" Her reaction worried me.
She had never done anything like this; on the contrary, she had
always woken up slowly . . . needing "enough time" to finally open
her eyes. But now she was sitting on the bed, talking fast.

"The principles are important!" she repeated. "Of course
they're important!"

The tone of her voice and the expression she had on her face made my concern turn into fear.

"Are you okay?" I asked her. "What's the matter with you?"

"The parchments!" she said to me. "Please hand them to me! Bring me a pen and paper too."

Immediately, we sat down on the sofa. Mary took the parchments and began to read the statements, only the titles, one by one, asking me to write them down.

I obeyed and wrote each sentence with the old fountain pen. When I had finished, she explained why.

"I saw them," she said, still deeply moved as her words came out in a gush. "I saw them clearly, and his hands were pointing to the principles."

"Wait!"

My fear had risen a level, and I put my hands on her shoulders, shaking her gently. "Calm down, please. Who did you see?"

"Rachel and our old pastor. They were both looking at me, and their faces were shining with a dazzling light. Then they bowed their heads, and with their hands they combined letters to form a sentence.

"What sentence did they write?" Curiosity now made me talk faster. I repeated my question: "Tell me! What sentence did they write?"

"The same one you will see if you take 'the beginning letters of the principles.'"

I looked at her, yet not understanding what she meant. Had the pressure she'd been under been so much that it had affected my wife's coherence?

She must have read my thoughts, or perhaps my look of confusion was comical, because she began to laugh as she took the sheet of paper on which I had written the principles and underlined some letters. Then she turned it toward me.

Only then did I begin to understand.

I read the fifteen statements again, and I concentrated on *the first letters of the principles.*

Then I got it. By combining the underlined letters, I saw a sentence that made sense. Tremendous sense!*

> *Everything starts with loving God.*
>
> *Watch over and preserve the health of your family.*
>
> *Spend quality time with your Bible.*
>
> *You either love those you serve, or you will stop serving them.*
>
> *You are valuable.*
>
> *Be willing to forgive others and yourself as well.*
>
> *Always stay grounded and levelheaded. After your greatest triumphs remember that your feet are still made of clay.*
>
> *Pray. Speak to God and let Him speak to you. Make this a habit.*
>
> *Laugh when you can; do it daily.*
>
> *Greatness is knowing how to be humble.*
>
> *Respond faithfully to the One who has chosen you.*
>
> *Learn the tremendous value of trials and difficulties.*
>
> *Changes in the night? Never! Wait for morning to come.*

---

*   In the original language of this book—Spanish—the acrostic formed by the first letter of each sentence forms the sentence in Spanish: Everything is by grace!

Honesty: a highly prized value in heaven and earth.

Learn to create a team.

Mary took the small paper that had appeared in the bottom of the chest and read it again: "When life turns hard, and darkness hovers around you; when the slope seems too steep and the weight becomes too much, return to these principles. The last ones are crucial, but the first ones are too . . ."

My voice now responded like an answer, reciting the sentence that I had written:

"Everything is by grace."

I looked at Mary and repeated it again. I then closed my eyes and recited it again. I thought about the fear I had woken up with early this morning. The feeling of being an orphan overwhelmed me, and my expectations that were filled with fear made me shudder . . . and I repeated it.

I took Mary's hand, and together we fell back down on the mattress with our eyes fixed on the ceiling.

It was no longer dark. Dawn had finally come.

And dawn had come inside us too . . . The shadows had retreated, scared off by the radiant light of the truth: almost nothing depends on me, because everything depends on Him.

A little while later, Mary sat up again in the bed. She wrapped her arms around her legs and looked at the parchments.

"What do you plan on doing with these?" she asked me.

"To live the principles they contain."

"Nothing more?"

"And nothing less."

She smiled, intrigued.

"What more do you want me to do?"

She looked at me, thoughtful. Then she turned her face to the parchments and then looked at me again.

"They contain too much wisdom; it's too much wealth to keep it locked up in this big chest."

I knew she had a plan in mind, but I don't like playing guessing games.

"What more do you think I should do?"

She lay down beside me and turned toward me, wrapping her arm around my waist, and did not take her eyes off me.

"The chapter of your life that you have just closed could be called *Mondays with My Old Pastor*." Her honest and sincere smile was the same one that won me over the first time I saw it. "Don't you think it's time to begin a time in your life in which you transfer the wealth you've received?"

I looked at her, thinking. I stared at the ceiling again, pondering, and then I quickly sat up in bed.

It was Mary now who looked at me startled.

"Mondays with my young disciples!" I didn't say it; I proclaimed it.

"That sounds good."

I nodded in agreement and repeated: "From 'Mondays with my old pastor' to 'Mondays with my young disciples.' It's a wise transition. It will be an exciting new phase."

One by one I put the parchments back in the chest and then closed it. As I held it in my hand, it felt as if it was burning. There was no doubt; it was time to pass on these principles and wisdom.

"Yes," I said to Mary. "It will be an exciting new phase."

"It won't be easy," she warned me, "but when the slope seems too steep and the weight too much—"

"Then we will remember . . ." I interrupted her.

We joined our voices together and we both declared: "Everything is by grace, which will sustain us forever!"

Conclusion

Everything Is by Grace

I started this book when a thought emerged from a crevice in my mind: *Perhaps I should dedicate myself to something else.* I finish it now with the firm decision of dedicating myself to one thing: keeping the cross held up high, and continuing, with all possible dignity, the sublime work that has been entrusted to me.

My thoughts came together, and I accepted the reality that God has given me *one* light and *one* place where to unfold it. *One* horse to gallop with, and *one* destination to aim for.

In the nocturnal heavens there are not only planets, suns, and shining moons but also stars, including ones called dwarfs. Even small points, without any pretension, give off light in the extreme darkness of outer space.

I have come to the conclusion that victory and, above all, happiness do not lie in being a shining star, but rather being who

God meant you to be and shining your tiny bit of light in the place He has chosen for you.

The forests would be silent if the only birds that sang were the ones that knew how to do it the best. The symphony of a forest, the beauty of this symphony, is made up of the multiplicity of songs, where lofty notes are sung along with cacophonous sounds, but when joined together, they all create a healing therapy for the oppressed soul.

During the night, a person asks a thousand questions. The dark nights of the soul are really something!

But morning finally comes, and the sun restores everything to its rightful place. Then we discover that the grotesque shadows at night that seemed like arms of a skeleton were only branches laden with fruit, and that empty blackness that seemed like an abyss in the darkness was a well of crystal-clear water willing to refresh us.

Khalil Gibran, the Lebanese poet, hit it on the head when he said that "in the heart of every *winter* lives spring, behind the veil of every night is a dawn that is smiling."

Perhaps you have come out of a desert, or perhaps you are drawing near to one. Or it may be in this exact moment your feet are stuck in the burning sand of a dune.

No matter what it is, seek after the cross.

There is a cross in every desert, and in its shade will appear the most refreshing oasis that you can imagine.

You will drink until you are full, and resting on its soft wood, you will look life square in the face and come to the conclusion that it's worth going on, because . . .

EVERYTHING IS BY GRACE.

Notes

The Second Monday

1. Original Spanish story from José Carlos Bermejo, *Regálame la Salud de un Cuento* (Santander, España: Sal Terrae, 2004), 74.

The Third Monday

1. Original Spanish story from A. Cruz Beauregard, *Cápsulas Motivacionales* (Editorial Diana, 1988).
2. Story by Shel Silverstein, *The Giving Tree* (New York: Harper & Row, 1964), Spanish translation taken from José Carlos Bermejo, *Regálame la Salud de un Cuento* (Santander, España: Sal Terrae, 2004).
3. Bermejo, *Regálame la Salud.*

The Fourth Monday

1. José Carlos Bermejo, *Regálame la Salud de un Cuento* (Santander, España: Sal Terrae, 2004).

The Fifth Monday

1. Quote is attributed to Rabindranath Tagore, to Khalil Gibram, and to Lao-Tsé, http://forum.wordreference.com/showthread.php?t=1829209.

The Sixth Monday

1. Jorge Bucay, *Déjame que te cuente: Los cuentos que me enseñaron a vivir* (Rba Bolsillo, 2005).

The Ninth Monday

1. Original Spanish story from José Carlos Bermejo, *Regálame la Salud de un Cuento* (Santander, España: Sal Terrae, 2004), 69.

The Tenth Monday

1. Original Spanish quote from Pearl S. Buck, http://es.wikiquote.org/wiki/Pearl_S._Buck.
2. From James C. Hunter, *La Paradoja* (Ediciones Urano S.A Colección Empresa Activa, 1999).

The Eleventh Monday

1. Original Spanish story from José Carlos Bermejo, *Regálame la Salud de un Cuento* (Santander, España: Sal Terrae, 2004), 26.

The Twelfth Monday

1. The story the old pastor tells here was inspired by a true story of Dr. Jesse Miranda, which is told in his book *Leadership and Friendship* (Grand Rapids, MI: Vida Publishers, 1998).

About the Author

José Luis Navajo did his studies in the Seminario Evangélico Español, the Asociación de Formación Teológica Evangélica, and the Escuela Bíblica Salem. Today he is part of the pastoral team of the Salem Evangelical Church in Madrid, Spain. The pastoral ministry is his calling and vision: his other great vocation is literature, as he is an author of several books. He gives conferences, participates as a commentator on different radio programs, and is a column writer. He and his wife, Gene, have two daughters, Querit and Miriam.